DOCTOR FAUSTUS
1616

THE MALONE SOCIETY
REPRINTS, VOL. 186
2019

PUBLISHED FOR THE MALONE SOCIETY
BY MANCHESTER UNIVERSITY PRESS

Altrincham Street, Manchester M1 7JA, UK
www.manchesteruniversitypress.co.uk

British Library Cataloguing-in-Publication Data
A catalogue record for this book is available from the British Library

Library of Congress Cataloging-in-Publication Data applied for

ISBN 978–1–5261–2387–9

Typeset by New Leaf Design, Huttons Ambo, North Yorkshire

Printed in the UK by Henry Ling Limited, at the Dorset Press, Dorchester, DT1 1HD

This edition of *Doctor Faustus 1616* was prepared by Chiaki Hanabusa and checked by Eric Rasmussen, with additional bibliographical assistance from G. R. Proudfoot and H. R. Woudhuysen. The editor wishes to express his thanks to Paul Dean for comments on style. Completion of the edition was facilitated by the award of the Bibliographical Society's Fredson Bowers Award for 2015–16.

The Society is grateful to the British Library for permission to reproduce its unique copy of the play (C.34.d.26).

March 2019   PAUL DEAN

CONTENTS

INTRODUCTION

THE 1616 QUARTO

Christopher Marlowe's *The Tragical History of the Life and Death of Doctor Faustus* (1616; STC 17432) was published for John Wright, bookseller in London. No printer is named. The text of the 1616 edition has traditionally been labelled the 'B-text', and this first B-text edition is the fourth quarto of the play (hereafter Q4).[1] In 1604, Thomas Bushell had published the first 'A-text' quarto edition (Q1) printed by Valentine Simmes (STC 17429). Subsequently, Wright published Q2 (1609; STC 17430) and Q3 (1611; STC 17431) printed by George Eld. On 13 September 1610, Wright was assigned by Bushell the rights of ownership of 'The tragicall history of the horrible life & death of Do^r. ffaustus, written by C. M:' upon the payment of six pence.[2] Wright's caution about how well Q2 would sell might have caused him to delay purchasing Bushell's right to the play until a year after he published it.[3] Assured of the play's popularity, Wright proceeded a year later to the publication of Q3, and went on to acquire the manuscript of the revised and expanded B-text for Q4. By the time he retired in 1640–1, Wright had published Q5 (1619; STC 17433), Q6 (1620; 17434), Q7 (1624; 17435), Q8 (1628; 17435.5), and Q9 (1631; 17436), each reprinted from its predecessor. The publisher's advertisement, 'With new Additions.', was printed for the first time on the title-page of Q5.

The only surviving copy of Q4 is in the British Library (C.34.d.26). Q4 collates 4°: A–H⁴. The title-page is A1ʳ. The full title reads 'The Tragicall History | of the Life and Death | of *Doctor Faustus*. | Written by *Ch. Mar.*'.[4] Below it is the famous large woodcut depicting Faustus standing within a magic circle with a book and a wand in his hands, and Mephistopheles appearing in front of him through the floor of Faustus's study. The width of this page

---

[1] For bibliographical details of both the A- and the B-text editions of the play, see W. W. Greg, *A Bibliography of the English Printed Drama to the Restoration*, 4 vols (London, 1939–59), 1.327–31 (no. 205 (*a–j*)). *STC* references are to Alfred W. Pollard and G. R. Redgrave, *A Short-Title Catalogue of Books Printed in England, Scotland, and Ireland and of English Books Printed Abroad 1475–1640*, 2nd edn, revised and enlarged by W. A. Jackson, F. S. Ferguson, and Katharine F. Pantzer, 3 vols (London, 1976–91), 2.139. See also Martin Wiggins with Catherine Richardson, *British Drama 1533–1642: A Catalogue: Volume II: 1567–1589* (Oxford, 2012), pp. 419–27 (no. 810); 'ESTC: English Short Title Catalogue', British Library Website (http://www.bl.uk/).

[2] Greg, *Bibliography*, 1.26. See also Edward Arber, *A Transcript of the Registers of the Company of Stationers of London, 1554–1640 A.D.*, 5 vols (London and Birmingham, 1875–94), 3.442.

[3] For Wright's prudent practice in publishing plays, see pp. xxxi–xxxiii.

[4] In this Introduction and elsewhere, long-s and ligatures are not reproduced; black-letter is reproduced in roman, while roman and italic/swash are reproduced in roman and italic, respectively. On the title-page of the unique copy of Q4, the author's abbreviated name '*Ch. Mar.*' has been wrongly expanded by pen and ink to '*Ch. Mar*klin.'.

was probably miscalculated by the compositor, and, as a result, the right-hand side of the woodcut, including parts of a cross and Mephistopheles's body, was cropped at the edge in the BL copy in the course of later binding.[5] Unfortunately, the woodcut does not depict an actual scene from the theatre and, therefore, cannot constitute a record of the play's performance. Notwithstanding, this woodcut, dominating the centre of the title-page and perhaps attracting attention to the play in bookshops, became an icon for the play when Q4 was published; it was used on each subsequent edition up to 1631.[6] Below it on the Q4 title-page is the imprint, '*LONDON*, | Printed for *Iohn Wright*, and are to be sold at his shop | without Newgate, at the sig<ne> of the | Bibl<e.> 1616.'.[7] Sig. A1ᵛ is blank. At the head of A2ʳ is a set of printer's flowers making up two rows, each of nine flowers. Below them is the head-title, reading 'THE | TRAGEDIE OF | Doctor Faustus.', itself followed by a rule. The main text begins at TLN 12 with a centred stage direction, 'Enter Chorus.'. The Chorus's speech begins with the upper-case roman letter 'N' (9.0 × 10.0 millimetres); its height is slightly longer than two lines of text. The text ends at TLN 2132 on H3ᵛ, immediately followed by the same Latin motto as appears in Q1, 'Terminat hora diem, Terminat Author opus.' (The hour ends the day, the author ends his work). The final line of the page reads '*F I N I S.*' (TLN 2134). The unique copy lacks leaf H4, which was presumably blank.

Q4 is not divided into acts or scenes. The least intrusive editorial division of the play would be as follows: Chorus 1, Scenes 1–5, Chorus 2, Scenes 6–7, Chorus 3, Scenes 8–19, and Chorus 4.[8] Although Scene 7 (of Robin's book-stealing episode) has been considered misplaced,[9] and Chorus 2 is merely a shorter version of Chorus 3, the B-text as it is preserved in Q4 was what Jacobean and Caroline readers actually read. In modern critical editions, the act and scene divisions can vary slightly, according to the editor's judgement; Chorus 2 is often omitted.

Each page of sheets A–D has thirty-eight text-lines, including blank lines between speech and stage directions but excluding the direction line. The depth of the text area, excluding the headline and the direction line, measures 156–8 millimetres. In sheets E–H, the compositors reduced the number of

[5] In all subsequent editions, Q5–Q9, the entire image is visible.

[6] It was also lent to Henry Gosson, publisher, in 1628 (the year Q8 was issued by Wright), for use on the broadside ballad, *The Tragedy of Doctor Lamb* ([1628]; STC 19272).

[7] The 'ne' of 'signe' and 'e.' of 'Bible.' were conjectured by Greg (*Bibliography*, 1.328).

[8] TLN references for this division of the scenes are: Chorus 1 (12–39), Scene 1 (40–199), Scene 2 (200–35), Scene 3 (236–350), Scene 4 (351–99), Scene 5 (400–567), Chorus 2 (568–79), Scene 6 (580–753), Scene 7 (754–87), Chorus 3 (788–812), Scene 8 (813–1137), Scene 9 (1138–91), Scene 10 (1192–381), Scene 11 (1382–499), Scene 12 (1500–33), Scene 13 (1534–87), Scene 14 (1588–647), Scene 15 (1648–784), Scene 16 (1785–95), Scene 17 (1796–904), Scene 18 (1905–2103), Scene 19 (2104–23), and Chorus 4 (2124–32).

[9] See Roy T. Eriksen, 'The Misplaced Clownage-Scene in *The Tragedie of Doctor Faustus* (1616) and Its Implications for the Play's Total Structure', *English Studies*, 62 (1981), 249–58, p. 250; *Doctor Faustus: A- and B-Texts (1604, 1616)*, ed. David Bevington and Eric Rasmussen (Manchester, 1993), pp. 287–8.

text-lines on each page to thirty-seven, with the depth of the page shrinking to 150–4 millimetres, accordingly. After the setting of sheet D was finished, the compositors probably cast-off the text once again to re-estimate how many pages the remaining text would need to be neatly accommodated. In other words, they wished to know where the final printed page of sheet H would end and how many lines of text would be left for that page. They had to avoid either the printed text overflowing sheet H or the setting finishing clumsily at the start of the sheet, for instance, on sig. H1^r or H1^v. If the text overflowed the final sheet, the printer would have to renegotiate a further supply of paper with Wright.[10] On the other hand, if six or seven out of eight pages of sheet H became uselessly blank, this would result in serious waste of paper. The compositors could have selected half-sheet imposition for sheet H, but, as it reduces by half the demand for paper, it would have caused a considerable deviation from the amount of paper that the publisher originally estimated.[11] Perhaps the compositors envisaged that, if they kept setting thirty-eight lines per page from E1^r to H3^r (saving some twenty-nine lines in current layout), the final page, H3^v, with only twenty-two lines plus '*F I N I S.*' at present, would have been blank. To avoid that happening, from E1^r they started to set thirty-seven lines per page. The blank final leaf H4 was probably turned back when all sheets were gathered and folded to cover the title-page as a wrapper.[12]

The width of the printer's measure is normally 92–4 millimetres in sheets A–H, although on a couple of pages, sigs A3^r and A3^v, it measures 95 millimetres, due perhaps to variation in paper shrinkage. The text is mainly set in a pica black-letter fount, called 'textura', with twenty lines measuring 82–3 millimetres. In the first quarter of the sixteenth century, English printers adopted the northern French textura directly from France or Flanders, and the textura gradually became established in England as the ordinary standard black-letter type.[13] An 82-millimetre fount of pica roman was used for stage directions, speech-prefixes, Latin, and most proper names.[14] Also printed in roman are 'all promises' made between Faustus and Mephistopheles (TLN 499–513 and part of 514), Mephistopheles's English charm to make Faustus invisible (1040–8), and the dirge that the friars sing (1126–35). Italic is rarely used, and only for emphasis in some (but not all) roman passages, as roman is used for emphasis against textura. Thus, the title-page is mostly roman, but has '*Doctor Faustus*', '*Ch. Mar.*', '*LONDON*', and '*Iohn Wright*'. '*Thunder.*'

[10] Philip Gaskell, *A New Introduction to Bibliography* (Oxford, 1972), p. 41, states that casting-off enabled the compositor to make decisions about typographical details so that 'the text would not overrun the last whole sheet by a page or two'.

[11] For half-sheet imposition, see Gaskell, *New Introduction*, p. 83.

[12] Ronald B. McKerrow, *An Introduction to Bibliography for Literary Students* (Oxford, 1927), p. 123.

[13] H. D. L. Vervliet, *Sixteenth-Century Printing Types of the Low Countries* (Amsterdam, 1968), p. 42; A. F. Johnson, *Type Designs: Their History and Development*, 3rd edn (London, 1966), p. 10.

[14] The following are set in black-letter: part of the stage direction (TLN 1136–7), 'Lucifer' (323), 'Hungary' (1021), 'Germany' (1030), 'Millaine' (1089), 'France' (1094), and 'Greece' (1800, 1808).

and '*Faustus*' occur in a stage direction (TLN 236, and '*Thunder*,' at 253); the signature '*Iohn Faustus*' concludes his promises otherwise set in roman (514); an italic speech-prefix contrasts with Mephistopheles's line of Latin set in roman (646); and the text ends with italic '*F I N I S*.'.

The text of Q4 was set by two compositors, designated A and B. Robert Ford Welsh identified them on the basis of their habitual spellings, the use of the apostrophe in contracted words, and of ligatures such as 'ee' and 'oo'. The contrasting spellings that differentiate the work of the two compositors are 'deuil/diuel' (Compositor A/Compositor B), 'I'le/Il'e', 'Benuolio/Benvolio', 'go/goe', 'do/doe', and '-y/-ie'. Compositor A often used ''tis', 'e're', 'o're', and 'we'le/wee'le', but B preferred 'tis', 'ere', 'ore', and 'wee'l'. Compositor A only occasionally used the 'ee' and 'oo' ligatures, while B employed them frequently. The division of their stints determined by Welsh is as follows: Compositor A set sigs A3^v–D2^r (TLN 111–911), D3^r (950–85), E1^r–E2^v (1095–230), F2^v–G2^v (1484–790), and H2^v–H3^v (2040–134), while Compositor B set A2^r–A3^r (9–110), D2^v (912–49), D3^v–D4^v (986–1094), E3^r–F2^r (1231–483), and G3^r–H2^r (1791–2039).[15] In total, of all sixty pages from A2^r to H3^v, Compositor A set thirty-nine pages (65 per cent) and Compositor B set twenty-one (35 per cent). We do not know which of the two compositors set the title-page.

The first three leaves of each sheet were signed, except for the title-page on sig. A1^r. The signature numbers 2 and 3 are always Arabic, and the capital letters usually black-letter. Roman capitals, however, are used by the compositors when the catchword was part of a roman speech-prefix or roman stage direction (on C2^r, C3^r, D2^r, F2^r, F3^r, G2^r, and G3^r, but not on C1^r), or when the page-break occurred within roman text (on B1^r and E1^r; both set by Compositor A). The setting of the catchword is mostly accurate where it is sufficiently visible. In sheets A–D of the unique copy, the direction line at the foot of the page was often severely cropped; it is invisible on D4^v, while only small traces of type can be seen or adumbrated on A4^v, B2^r, B3^v, B4^r, B4^v, C2^v, C3^v, C4^v, and D3^v. A verbal disparity between the catchword and the first word of the following page can be observed in 'A' (catchword on E3^v; set by Compositor B) and 'Senit.' (stage direction on E4^r; B). The catchword is probably correct here, for a similar direction 'A Senit.' was used on E3^r (TLN 1244; B). The indefinite article was possibly dropped from the direction on E4^r by Compositor B. Typographical disparity can be seen between 'Ten' (catchword on H2^r; B) and 'ten' (the initial word on H2^v; A). An obvious misspelling of the catchword, 'Aawy' (set by A) for 'Away', occurs on B3^r. The catchword 'golde n' on G2^v (A) may have been caused by a space pulled out somewhere to the left of the catchword or by loose pressure from quads during the printing of the outer forme of sheet G, with 'golde' slightly shifted to the left.

As a rule, both compositors arranged longer stage directions (more than two lines) in an inverted pyramidal form (sigs B4^v, TLN 483–5; D2^r, 902–5;

[15] Robert Ford Welsh, 'The Printing of the Early Editions of Marlowe's Plays' (unpublished doctoral dissertation, Duke University, NC, 1964), pp. 129–45.

D4^r, 1023–5; E3^r, 1244–7; E4^r, 1303–13; F2^v, 1500–3; G2^v, 1785–8). Another direction on F2^v (1496–9) was exceptionally set in the usual prose form, possibly to avoid two successive pyramidal stage directions. Compositor A often used space-saving techniques to prevent the text from overflowing the line. Where he had to turn-over a speech for lack of space, he employed either turn-downs or turn-ups. The former occur four times, on B3^r (376–7), B4^r (453–4), C2^v (647–8), and C3^r (669–70), while the latter can be seen five times, on B1^v (291–2), B3^r (408–9), B4^r (451–2), C4^v (772–3), and F4^r (1603–4). The compositors' norm was, it seems, to set a blank line both above and below the stage direction except for exit/exeunt directions (12, 107, 200, etc.). They frequently deviated from this standard by omitting a blank line that should be set below the direction (658, 665, etc.) or both blanks to be set above and below (40, 261, 547, 758, etc.) to save space. When setting a short direction, they often set it in the right-hand margin after the speech line for space saving (100, 137–8, 428, etc.). Compositor A seems to have avoided wasting space by setting Mephistopheles's extremely short replies, 'Meph. In hell.' (B2^r, 310) and 'Meph. I.' (C2^v, 637), on lines that already contain speeches. Exit/exeunt directions were also often set in a shortened form; Compositor A used 'Ex.A.' (C3^r, 662) and Compositor B set 'Ex.Fa.& Mep.' (D3^v, 1018). By contrast, the compositors sometimes wasted space by inserting two blank lines above the stage direction as on C2^r (592; set by A) or both above and below the direction as on G2^v (1785–8; A). They also inserted a textually unnecessary blank line before the stage direction at the head of the page as on D4^r(B), E4^r(B), and F2^v (A), while Compositor B omitted it on G3^v to save space. On F2^v, Compositor A divided into a couple of lines a speech that could have been safely set in a single line (1510–11), as if to waste space. In all sheets, the compositors sometimes saved space, but also wasted it whenever they found it necessary to do so. In other words, they were seeking to accommodate the text they were setting to follow the predetermined marks on the printer's manuscript. This indicates that the text had been cast-off in advance of composition, which in turn plausibly suggests that the text in all sheets was set by formes, not seriatim. The presence of tightly set pages without blank lines, such as G3^v (its facing page, G4^r, has one blank line), and of others very loosely composed with five blank lines, like F2^v (F3^r has two blank lines), strongly supports the probability that the text was set by formes from cast-off copy.

Some textual flaws were unavoidable. Misspellings include 'aad' (TLN 74; set by B), 'accdrd' (281; A), 'Dispath' (942; B), and 'Kaymond' (1099; A). There are turned letters, for instance, 'A[n]d' (679; A), 'co[m]e' (725; A), and '[m]en' (918; B). The compositors' botched work includes double punctuation marks 'Chaire.,' (1002; A), omission of punctuation marks after a speech (648; A, 752; A), after a stage direction (2005; B, 2094; A), and after a speech-prefix (1684; A, 1815; B, 1817; B, 1819; B), and the use of lower-case type at the beginning of a verse line (2040; A). The use of a full stop instead of a question mark (1176; A, 1200; A) may have been either the result of Compositor A's error or the influence of the printer's manuscript copy. A missing speech-prefix for Mephostopheles on B3^v (430; A) has been supplied in the left-hand margin of the BL copy in the form of a handwritten 'M.'. The compositors frequently used an ampersand where it became necessary for justification of a full line or of a prose speech (79, 208, 217, 255–7, 259, etc.). Compositor B used it when setting short stage directions in a narrow blank space after a verse speech on D3ᵛ and F2ʳ (1018, 1465). To justify full lines, the compositors also employed such abbreviated forms as 'yᵗ' (227, 1805) and 'cõfort' (1850). In addition to dashes (69, 655, 1572, 1577, etc.) and brackets (218, 1402), '&c.' appears twice in a verse speech (67, 77). Dashes, brackets, and '&c.', presumably, have nothing to do with justification; they may reflect the printer's copy-text.[16]

The paper used to print sheets E–H of the BL copy had a crease on its surface, which caused a slightly warped type impression. This is noticeable at TLN 1251: 1288, 1469: 1502, 1536: 1571, 1605: 1642, 1675: 1708, 2099: 2132. Paper flaws caused by silverfish (and their repairs) frequently affected the text. A hole, now repaired, by a bookworm affects the reading of 'Glut.' at 733. Modern conservation work obscured parts of readings at 695–6, 711–13, 770–1, and 917.[17] Perhaps flaking of tiny pieces of paper rag damaged the surface of sig. A2ᵛ, with minor loss of text at 51–4. An unclear phenomenon affected the readings at 105–6 (it may have been caused by human hairs). Locally heavy pressure from the press produced an inked quad (184) and an inked space (1023), while the presswork on the thin paper produced a number of instances of show-through on C1ᵛ and C4ʳ. A large stain is visible in the outer margins on E2ʳ and E2ᵛ.[18]

Welsh identified five damaged types recurring from B(o) to C(o).[19] Although the number of identified types was small, he concluded on the basis of the five types that recurred from B(o) to C(o) that sheets B–C were printed in the order of B(o)–B(i)–C(o)–C(i).[20] Due to the lack of a sufficient amount of type-recurrence evidence, the printing order of the other sheets was unknown to him.

[16] A two-line brace is also used on F2ʳ (TLN 1465–6), but it is hard to determine whether it reflects the printer's copy or is Compositor B's expedient.
[17] The text at TLN 695–6, 711–13, and 770–1 is visible on EEBO and in the Scolar Press facsimile edition, Christopher Marlowe, *Doctor Faustus 1604 and 1616* (Menston, 1970). Presumably the unique copy was repaired after it was filmed and photographed for the facsimile. Repair work at TLN 917 (sig. D2ᵛ) slightly affects the reading of 'know'st' at 881 (D2ʳ).
[18] For lost or damaged readings, see the list of 'Obscured and Damaged Readings' below, pp. xliii–xlvi.
[19] Outer formes are referred to by the signature letter followed by '(o)'; inner formes by the letter followed by '(i)'. The black-letter types that he identified were 'm' ('somewhat', sig. B4ᵛ, TLN 481; 'more', C2ᵛ, 645), 'p' ('Leapes', B1ʳ, 240; 'pardon', C3ʳ, 676), 'r' ('dinner', B1ʳ, 223; 'fresh', C2ᵛ, 636), 'H' ('Had' B2ᵛ, 338; 'Hell', C1ʳ, 524), and 'S' ('Starres', B1ʳ, 249; 'Starres', C2ᵛ, 624). A check of all these types in the original copy revealed that 'm' and 'H' were precisely identified, while the rest of the types may be identified with a slight degree of doubt. Welsh was unable to detect types recurring from B(i) to C(i).
[20] Welsh, 'The Printing of the Early Editions', p. 150. Out of seventeen types Welsh identified throughout the text, no type was found recurring from B(i) to C(o). This negative evidence, although weak in itself, may also support the printing order proposed by Welsh.

xiv

Compositor B, who set sigs H1^v and H2^r, two of the three pages in H(i), had a serious shortage of roman upper-case 'F's. The number of roman 'F's (roman numerals in the table below) and of italic '*F*'s (italic numerals) used in sheets F–H, with assignments of stints to compositors, is as follows:

	Outer forme				Total	Inner forme				Total
Sheet F	1^r	2^v	3^r	4^v		1^v	2^r	3^v	4^r	
	8	7/*1*	7	3	25/*1*	8	9	8	2	27
Compositor	B	A	A	A		B	B	A	A	
Sheet G	1^r	2^v	3^r	4^v		1^v	2^r	3^v	4^r	
	4	4	5/*1*	6	19/*1*	6	11	12	4/*1*	33/*1*
Compositor	A	A	B	B		A	A	B	B	
Sheet H	1^r	2^v	3^r			1^v	2^r	3^v		
	20	7	4		31	2/*13*	0/*3*	3/*1*		5/*17*
Compositor	B	A	A			B	B	A		

As soon as Compositor B exhausted all roman 'F's on the third line of H1^v (TLN 1970), where he used the final two, he inevitably started to substitute its italic equivalent thirteen times there and three times again on H2^r. The type-shortage was clearly caused by the frequent references to 'Faustus' and by a large number of his speech-prefixes in G(i) and H(o), where sixty-four roman 'F's in total were set.[21] The high demand for the roman 'F's and the consequent type-shortage make it certain that G(i) was printed after G(o), because this order (rather than the reverse) better explains the shortage of roman 'F's in H(i), as is discussed below.

It is usually assumed that, when only a single press was used, distribution of the finished forme began shortly after the start of the presswork of the forme that would immediately follow it, and that by this time the composition of the forme that would follow the forme at the press would have already started.[22] The composition of H(o) and H(i) was, however, finished more speedily, because they had only three pages each. It is, therefore, plausible to think that, when Compositor B started composition of sig. H1^v, G(i) was still at the press, and that H(o) had already been brought to the imposing stone. In this situation, all sixty-four roman 'F's were unavailable to B while he was setting H1^v and H2^r, and he was thus forced to use its italic equivalent sixteen times on the two pages. When the presswork of G(i) was finished, the roman 'F's in its distributed pages started to replenish the type-case. Compositor

---

[21] There are plenty of conversations between Faustus and the Carter (on sig. G2^r), Faustus and the Old Man (G3^v), and Faustus and the Three Scholars (H1^r). Calls to Faustus by the Old Man and by the Three Scholars as well as Faustus's self-reflexive calls also increased demand for roman 'F's.

[22] For the use of only one press, see the running-title analysis and the printer identification below.

A could now set up the main text of the final page, H3^v, using three of these and 'F I N I S.', using an italic 'F'. If this conjectural sequence of events is accurate, sheets G–H were printed by a single press in the order G(o)–G(i)–H(o)–H(i), and, in H(i), Compositors A and B worked consecutively, not concurrently. It is not clear why, in a roman stage direction on F2^v (TLN 1496), '*Faustus*' alone was set in italic type. The reason for the initial italic '*F*' type substitutions, '*Faustus*' on G3^r (1806) and '*Faust.*' on G4^r (1885), is also unclear, but they may perhaps have been caused by foul case rather than by a local type-shortage.[23]

The running-titles, or headlines, start on sig. A2^v. Set in large roman type, they read 'The Tragicall Historie' on verso pages and 'Of Doctor Faustus.' on recto pages. There are no spelling variants throughout the book. Only partial analysis of the running-titles is possible, since in sheets A and G–H some of them were either severely or slightly trimmed, to the extent that most or part of the type impression was removed. On A3^r, the running-title was entirely cropped, and only the lower bowl of 'g' in 'Tragicall' is clearly visible on A3^v. The upper part of the running-title has been trimmed on A2^v, G2^r, G2^v, H2^r, and H3^v, while only part of it can be seen on A4^r, G3^v, and H3^r. The sole identifiable damaged type is an upper-case 'F' in 'Faustus.' that has a tiny broken fragment of type sticking out from the stem under the lower arm. This slightly broken letter first appears on B3^r and B4^r and regularly reappears on sigs 3^r and 4^r in sheets C–G,[24] but it has not been detected in sheets A and H. The limited evidence available suggests that sheets B–G were printed with a single skeleton used successively for both formes, and were accordingly printed by a single press. Another recto running-title can be identified on both G2^r in G(i) and H2^r in H(i). It has a relatively wider gap between the 'D' and the 'o' in 'Doctor' caused by the loosening of type or of a space during the presswork. This identification suggests that the same set of running-titles was used for G(i) and the three pages in H(i), and that H(i) was, therefore, printed using part of the same skeleton forme employed for sheets B–G. Based on the fact that the gap in 'Doctor' first appeared while G(i) was being machined, and that it reappears not in H(o) but in H(i), it can be deduced that a different set of running-titles was arranged for use in H(o). As has already been discussed, H(o) was brought to the imposing stone earlier than expected, and while G(i) was still at the press, the compositors, probably to save time, set up new running-titles for the three pages in H(o). The limited evidence suggests that sheets B–H were printed by a single press, with a single skeleton forme used in both formes of sheets B–G and H(i); H(o) was imposed with a different skeleton forme,

[23] Foul case may also have been the cause of the single italic '*F*' in '*Faustus*' on sig. E3^v (TLN 1297).

[24] Its identification on sig. C3^r is less certain, owing to the relatively weak impression of the letter.

using a new set of running-titles. Lacking reliable evidence, it is impossible to determine anything useful about the running-titles in sheet A.[25]

Survival of only a single copy severely limits the scope of investigation of the quarto's watermarks. Unfortunately, only a small part of a 'pot' watermark has been identified, and in fewer than half the expected number of leaves, namely, leaves A1, C3, D2, E1, F2, G4, and H3.[26] No mark is visible in sheet B. From this extremely limited evidence, all that can be deduced is that the unique copy may have been printed with paper imported from Normandy or elsewhere in northern or central France, where 'pots' were among the favourite watermark designs in paper mills in the early seventeenth century.[27]

The printer of Q4, unnamed in the title-page imprint as mentioned above, has not hitherto been identified. The main reason for this is that, apart from the impressive woodcut on the title-page and a small set of printer's flowers on sig. A2ʳ, no printer's device, ornament, or ornamental initials that can safely be used to identify the printer appear in the quarto. The only remaining clues are damaged types. To identify the printer using such evidence, it is essential to demonstrate that distinctive damaged types, bent, cracked, or broken, unmistakably detected in Q4, also appear in books printed by a known printer in or around 1616. By this means, the distinctive types can 'provide absolute evidence of the identity […] of the unknown printer of an unsigned book'.[28]

Research, therefore, started by looking for types with clearly identifiable damage in Q4 itself. In the light of previous experience with type identification, it seemed best to concentrate on pica roman rather than textura types, for black-letter types were sturdier and pica roman was more easily damaged. First, all battered roman types were closely examined, and more than a dozen types, both minuscule and majuscule, with evident flaws were detected, and their details sketched. The hard-and-fast principle here is that the more peculiar and conspicuous the damage, the more valuable and helpful it becomes, especially when the number of identified types is small. The reappearance of any of these types within the text of Q4 was also examined; if a damaged type recurs, it is possible to confirm the damage more precisely. In the end, for the printer identification, three type-pieces from Q4 were selected: two upper-case letters 'B' and 'M' and a lower-case 'n' (see the Appendix). To conduct the type identification precisely, types were selected that showed evidence of more than a single trace of heavy damage. The 'B' has a very large crack, not only in

---

[25] The conclusion reached here differs from that of Welsh ('The Printing of the Early Editions', pp. 145–50), who claimed to have identified two skeletons from his research, using a reproduction of Q4 on microfilm.

[26] As the watermark was wired in the middle space at the left-hand side of the paper mould, it should normally be visible in two of four quarto leaves per sheet at the narrow gutter of the bound book. See Gaskell, *New Introduction*, pp. 57–77.

[27] Edward Heawood, *Watermarks Mainly of the 17th and 18th Centuries* (Hilversum, 1950; repr. 1957), pp. 24, 26.

[28] Adrian Weiss, 'Bibliographical Methods for Identifying Unknown Printers in Elizabethan/ Jacobean Books', *Studies in Bibliography*, 44 (1991), 183–228, p. 203. See also G. Thomas Tanselle, 'The Use of Type Damage as Evidence in Bibliographical Description', *The Library*, 5th series, 23 (1968), 328–51, p. 330.

the lower part of the stem, but in the lower bowl, while the 'n' has a large crack in the upper part of the left stem (immediately below the upper serif) and in the lower part of the right stem. This lower-case type appears twice in Q4, so that the precise nature of its damage can be confirmed from two images. On the other hand, the 'M' is only damaged in the lower-left serif, but it shows an extremely distinctive deformation that can rarely be found elsewhere. The selection of the two upper-case sorts follows the recognition that upper-case types in general 'often offer clearer and more reliable kinds of damage than lower-case letters'.[29] Although the three selected types are small in number, their damage is sufficiently distinctive to identify a printing-house.

The investigation began in the British Library, with a search for the three damaged types in books printed in London around 1616. The foremost candidate for the printer of Q4 was George Eld, who, in addition to Q2 and Q3 *Faustus*, had printed a wide variety of books since 1606 for (or to be sold by) Wright. Among these are *The Second Part of the Return from Parnassus* (1606; STC 19309–10), William Shakespeare's *Sonnets* (1609; STC 22353–3a), and Q2 of Thomas Dekker's *The Shoemakers' Holiday* (1610; STC 6524). In search of the damaged types, all pages, line by line, from type to type, were examined in the British Library copies of fifteen books that Eld produced in 1615–17,[30] but without result. The search for the types then moved to another fifteen books printed by George Purslowe, who is thought to have printed three editions of *Mucedorus* (1626, [1629?], 1631; STC 18238–9) for Wright. This second search was also fruitless. The third and final target printer was Nicholas Okes. The possibility of finding the three damaged types in Okes's books seemed slim, for the links between the two stationers appear slight; Okes is known to have printed only four books for Wright (as far as can be determined from imprints).[31] The examination, however, successfully uncovered the sorts in seven titles produced during 1615–18 with Okes's name as printer clearly present in the imprint, including Q4 of Dekker's *The Honest Whore* (1615; STC 6503) and Q2 of John Marston and others' *The Insatiate Countess* (1616; STC 17477).[32] On the one hand, the three damaged types were securely identified within the range of slightly variant type impressions, but on the other, the identical types on separate pages or in different books, or even in other copies of the same title, sometimes appear visibly dissimilar, due mainly to either heavy/weak inking or unsteady pressure from the press. To overcome this difficulty and to confirm the identifications more confidently, the search

[29] Antony Hammond, '*The White Devil* in Nicholas Okes's Shop', *Studies in Bibliography*, 39 (1986), 135–76, p. 161.
[30] Weiss, 'Bibliographical Methods', p. 206, observed that 'most pica fonts were replaced at intervals of about 2–4 years'.
[31] The four items comprise: Dekker's *Troia Nova Triumphans* (1612; STC 6530, printed by Okes, sold by Wright); Thomas Heywood's *The Four Prentices of London* (1615; STC 13321, printed [by Okes] for I[ohn]. W[right].); Arthur Dent's *A Sermon of God's Providence* (1616; STC 6649, printed [by Okes] for Wright); and Thomas Cooper's *The Cry and Revenge of Blood* (1620; STC 5698, printed by Okes for Wright).
[32] The seven titles were not produced by shared printing. Only in *The Insatiate Countess* is the printer's name abbreviated in the title-page imprint as '*N.O.*', but the full name is obvious.

continued at Oxford, using the Bodleian copies of Okes's books; six of the seven already known titles were examined and, as a result, the identifications were reconfirmed. In addition, one of the three types already found was detected in yet another book of Okes's that was unavailable in London. Copies in Cambridge University Library and Meisei University Library were also inspected to confirm these findings.[33] This research has made it clear that the printer of Q4 was Nicholas Okes.[34]

Some of Compositor A's habitual spellings closely correspond with those of a known compositor in Okes's printing-house. 'Compositor Y', identified by Robert K. Turner, Jr, was at work in Marston and others' Q2 *The Insatiate Countess* that was reprinted by Okes in the same year as Q4 *Faustus*.[35] Compositor Y is known to have favoured 'go' and 'do', as does Compositor A. The two compositors also share common spellings such as 'heere' and 'dore'; in Q4, the occurrences of the two spellings, four and three times respectively, fall exclusively in A's stints.[36] The spelling 'honour', which Y favoured, occurs five times in Q4; four of these were set by A.[37] There are, in general, ample instances of compositorial inconsistency in the spelling evidence used for compositor identification, but under the circumstances, it may not be too far-fetched to suggest that Welsh's Compositor A was probably identical with Turner's Compositor Y on the grounds that, of the five spellings with which Y was identified, four agree with A's habitual spellings, and that in the remaining single spelling A's share accounts for the majority of its occurrences. Yet another of Okes's compositors, identified by Philip Williams and Antony Hammond as 'Compositor A' in John Webster's Q1 *The White Devil* (1612; STC 25178), shared a preference with Welsh's A for the two spellings 'I'le' and '-y'. However, since Williams and Hammond's A favoured 'doe', the two workmen cannot be regarded as identical.[38]

[33] The sole instance of the negative identification was the 'B' examined on sig. O2^v/55 in the Cambridge copy of Samuel Daniel's *The Collection of the History of England* ([1618]; STC 6248), where it looked normal. Presumably, the type had been replaced before sheet O of this copy was printed. I am grateful to Professor Noriko Sumimoto for providing me with information on the Meisei copy of *The Honest Whore*. Later on, the 'B' sort was discovered in the present editor's copy of Arthur Hopton's *A Concordancy of Years* (1616; STC 13780). Okes's name is not in the imprint, but his printer's device with his initials 'N O' (McKerrow, 367) appears in the colophon, by which *STC* identified Okes as the printer of the entire book. See Ronald B. McKerrow, *Printers' & Publishers' Devices in England & Scotland 1485–1640* (London, 1913), p. 141.

[34] I am grateful to Peter W. M. Blayney, who kindly checked and confirmed my discussion and conclusion, and to Eric Rasmussen, who assisted me by communicating with him.

[35] Robert K. Turner, Jr, 'The Composition of *The Insatiate Countess*, Q2', *Studies in Bibliography*, 12 (1959), 198–203.

[36] The spelling 'heere/heere's' appears on sigs B4^v (TLN 479), C3^v (698), F4^r (1609), and G2^v (1765); 'dore/dores' occurs on E2^r (1192) and F2^v (1496, 1500). Compositor A also set 'heeretofore' on A4^r (176).

[37] Compositor A set 'honour' on sigs A3^r (TLN 92), A4^r (151), B3^v (421), and D1^v (869), but the same spelling on F1^v (1421) was set by B. Compositor A also set 'honourable' on F4^r (1585), but 'honour'd' on E3^r (1260) was set by B.

[38] Philip Williams, 'The Compositor of the "Pied Bull" *Lear*', *Studies in Bibliography*, 1 (1948–9), 61–8, p. 66; Hammond, '*The White Devil* in Nicholas Okes's Shop', pp. 135, 147, 154.

The running-title analysis suggests that sheets B–H of Q4 *Faustus* were printed on one press. In May 1615, Okes was one of five printers who were restricted by the Stationers' Company to owning only a single press, apart from an extra one, ready in the event of an emergency, such as mechanical troubles. Eight years later, in July 1623, he was still allowed only a single press.[39]

THE 1602 ADDITIONS

On 22 November 1602, Philip Henslowe, the manager of the Rose Theatre, paid four pounds to William Bird (Bourne) and Samuel Rowley for 'ther adicyones in docter fostes'.

> Lent vnto the companye the 22 of novmbȝ 1602
> to paye vnto wᵐ Bvrde & Samwell Rowle
> for ther adicyones in docter fostes the some of ⎬ iiij^li [40]

Between 1601 and 1603, a number of dramatists made additions to the Earl of Nottingham's (Admiral's) Men's plays, whether recent or old.[41] In 1601, Henslowe paid Ben Jonson forty shillings for 'his adicians' to Thomas Kyd's *The Spanish Tragedy*, and paid him again for writing his 'new adicyons' to it and a new play in 1602.[42] The same year, Thomas Dekker received forty shillings for 'new A dicyons', and again ten shillings for 'his adicions', to *Sir John Oldcastle*, while Thomas Heywood was paid twenty shillings for 'new a dicyons' to *Cutting Dick*. In 1603, a group of four dramatists, John Day, Richard Hathaway, Wentworth Smith, and 'the other poete', collected a total of forty shillings for 'ther adycyones' to *The Second Part of The Black Dog*.[43] Compared with what Henslowe paid other dramatists at about the same time, the sum paid to Bird and Rowley indicates that Q4 *Faustus* received more extensive additions than those provided for other plays.[44] Although Q1 *Faustus*

[39] Peter W. M. Blayney, *The Texts of 'King Lear' and their Origins: Volume I Nicholas Okes and the First Quarto* (Cambridge, 1982), pp. 40–1; *Records of the Court of the Stationers' Company 1602 to 1640*, ed. William A. Jackson (London, 1957), pp. 75, 158.

[40] *Henslowe's Diary*, ed. R. A. Foakes, 2nd edn (Cambridge, 2002), p. 206.

[41] The Admiral's Men were renamed Nottingham's Men from 22 October 1597, when their patron Charles Howard was created Earl of Nottingham, until about Christmas 1603, when the company was entitled Prince Henry's Men. See *Henslowe's Diary*, ed. Walter W. Greg, 2 vols (London, 1904–8), 2.334; E. K. Chambers, *The Elizabethan Stage*, 4 vols (Oxford, 1923), 2.186.

[42] Foakes, *Henslowe's Diary*, pp. 182, 203. The second payment cost Henslowe ten pounds in total. Notwithstanding these entries, the authorship of the additions is currently debated between Jonson and Shakespeare on stylistic grounds; see Douglas Bruster, 'Shakespearean Spellings and Handwriting in the Additional Passages Printed in the 1602 *Spanish Tragedy*', *Notes and Queries*, 258 (2013), 420–4; Will Sharpe, 'Authorship and Attribution', in *William Shakespeare and Others: Collaborative Plays*, ed. Jonathan Bate, Eric Rasmussen, *et al*. (Basingstoke, 2013), pp. 671–80.

[43] Foakes, *Henslowe's Diary*, pp. 213, 216, 223–4.

[44] Bird and Rowley had already written a play in collaboration. They received six pounds in December 1601, for finishing the rough draft of William Houghton's *Judas*; see Foakes, *Henslowe's Diary*, p. 185.

had only 1,518 lines of the main text, printed in forty-three quarto pages, Q4 has such substantial additions as to swell the text to over 2,120 lines in sixty-one pages. In other words, Q4 was rendered, apparently, over 600 lines and eighteen quarto pages longer than Q1 by Bird and Rowley's extensive revisions. The additions were evidently planned to coincide with Edward Alleyn's return to acting, as part of the celebrations for the opening of a new playhouse, the Fortune, built by Henslowe and Alleyn in Shoreditch in 1600.[45] Alleyn, the leading actor of the Admiral's/Nottingham's Men, who temporarily retired between 1597 and 1600, returned to the stage in 1601 (he finally left the Rose and the Fortune in 1604). Since Alleyn had most likely played the part of Faustus before his brief retirement, the newly revised *Doctor Faustus* would have been one of the most appropriate plays for revival and for the expectant fans who had hoped to see the leading player of the company performing the role once again.

In Q1 *Faustus*, approximately forty-seven characters, whether human, angelic, allegorical, or diabolical, appear. In the expanded text of Q4, the number swells to more than seventy-three, due to new farcical scenes and comic episodes introduced by the revisers.[46] Of all the named human characters in Q1 that reappear in Q4, only the second clown, 'Dick', is renamed: his name in Q1 was 'Rafe'.[47] This unique renaming could not have been accidental, nor would it have happened except as the result of the revisers' clear intentions. Richard 'Dick' Juby (or Jubie) was 'one of the principal boy actors' of the Admiral's/Nottingham's Men.[48] His name is recorded in four surviving theatrical 'plots' used by the company, namely, *Frederick and Basilea* (1597), *The Battle of Alcazar* (c. 1601), *The First Part of Tamar Cham* (c. 1601–2), and *The Second Part of Fortune's Tennis* (c. 1602).[49] In these plays, Juby played the following parts: Queen Basilea (*Frederick*), Queen Abdula Rais and a young banquet attendant (*Alcazar*), eight roles, including Chorus, attendant, messenger, and nobleman (*Tamar Cham*), and a child (*Tennis*).[50] In 1601–2, when three of the

[45] Roslyn L. Knutson, 'Influence of the Repertory System on the Revival and Revision of *The Spanish Tragedy* and *Dr. Faustus*', *English Literary Renaissance*, 18 (1988), 257–74, pp. 264–5. See also her 'Henslowe's Diary and the Economics of Play Revision for Revival, 1592–1603', *Theatre Research International*, 10 (1985), 1–18.

[46] Characters in unspecified numbers, such as Monks, Friars, Attendants, Soldiers, etc., have been counted as a minimum of two (see 'List of Roles', pp. xli–xlii).

[47] The devil 'Baliol' (Q1, TLN 415) was renamed 'Banio' (Q4, TLN 382) for unknown reasons. References to Q1 are to *Doctor Faustus 1604*, ed. Chiaki Hanabusa, Malone Society Reprints, 185 (Manchester, 2018).

[48] W. W. Greg, *Dramatic Documents from the Elizabethan Playhouses*, 2 vols (Oxford, 1931), Commentary, p. 67.

[49] Greg, *Dramatic Documents*, Commentary, pp. 123–37, 144–70; Foakes, *Henslowe's Diary*, pp. 328–33. It is evident that *Frederick* was performed on 3 June 1597 as a new play (Foakes, *Henslowe's Diary*, p. 58). For the dates of the other plots, see Wiggins, *British Drama*, 2.433 (*Alcazar*); Martin Wiggins with Catherine Richardson, *British Drama 1533–1642: A Catalogue: Volume III: 1590–1597* (Oxford, 2013), p. 136 (*Tamar Cham*); Martin Wiggins with Catherine Richardson, *British Drama 1533–1642: A Catalogue: Volume IV: 1598–1602* (Oxford, 2014), p. 274 (*Tennis*).

[50] Foakes, *Henslowe's Diary*, pp. 328–33.

four plays were staged, Juby was probably no longer very young, since by then he had a son who was baptized on 1 May 1602.[51] Perhaps he was in early youth with his voice still unbroken, and, presumably, he was sufficiently short and young-looking to play a child in *Tennis*. That the company assigned to him a number of roles, including the important one of Chorus in *Tamar Cham*, implies that the sharers and adult players trusted his gifts as a 'principal' boy actor. He was probably expected to become a popular and impressive young adult player, who would attract audiences and win their acclaim at the newly opened Fortune. There is no doubt that both Bird and Rowley were aware of his gifts, for they had a chance to watch his performance at close quarters: Bird's name appears in the plot of *Tamar Cham*, and Rowley acted with Juby in all of the four plays as described in their plots.

Asked by Henslowe to expand the A-text, the two player-playwrights may have felt no hesitation in proposing that the brilliant boy player should be cast in the revised *Faustus*, and the theatre manager appears to have had no reason to reject the idea.[52] Casting a boy player as the second clown released another adult comedian to be cast as a new farcical figure, the Carter.[53] Bird and Rowley also introduced a newly devised trick to enhance the comic effects by reversing the functions of Robin and Dick. In the cup-stealing scene of the B-text (TLN 1138–91), Mephistopheles tells Robin that he will be transformed into a dog and Dick into an ape, and orders Robin to 'carry him [Dick] vpon thy backe; away be gone.' (1179–88). Either wearing animal masks or with appropriate posture or movements, the two clowns were joyfully to leave the stage, with the adult Robin carrying the boy Dick on his back. In the A-text, however, it was Robin who was metamorphosed to an ape, while Rafe was turned into a dog (Q1, TLN 1042–3). In Q1, there is no speech or stage direction indicating Rafe's exit carrying Robin, the first clown, on his back, but if a similar action also took place in Q1, it would probably have provoked less amusement in the audience than the B-text performance, for in the former both characters were almost certainly played by adult comedians.[54] According to Thomas Pettitt,

> The exit of the clowns, the one riding on the other's back, is of course a familiar incident in the moral interludes and later derivatives […] where the Vice is carried off on the Devil's back, and similar ridings occur in folk drama.

[51] Chambers, *Elizabethan Stage*, 2.325.

[52] Greg stated that 'The reason for the change [of the name] is not apparent, for seeing that *Robin* is common to both texts, the names are unlikely to be those of actors', in *Marlowe's 'Doctor Faustus' 1604~1616: Parallel Texts*, ed. W. W. Greg, (Oxford, 1950), pp. 343–4. However, the variation of 'Rafe/Dick' seems to have nothing to do with the consistent use of 'Robin'.

[53] The stage direction 'Exeunt Clownes.' (TLN 1776) indicates that in addition to Robin and the Horse-Courser, the Carter was also played by an adult comedian.

[54] When, in Q1, Robin, the 'tall fellow in the round slop' (Q1, TLN 419), is insulted by being called 'boy' by Wagner (371), he sarcastically responds with 'I hope you haue seene many boyes with such pickadevaunts as I haue' (372–3). A reference in Thomas Wright's *The Passions of the Mind* (1601; STC 26039) indicates that at that time 'many Gentlemen' wore slops (sig. X5ᵛ). Rafe is pleased when Robin tells him that, by Robin's magic, he will be able to put Nan Spit freely 'to thy owne vse, as often as thou wilt, and at midnight' (Q1, 988).

The clown's riding can be seen in the *commedia dell'arte* and in German *Singspiele*, and it was, Pettitt continues, citing Peter Burke, part of 'a common European stock of dramaturgical formula[e]'.[55] Under the circumstances, watching the short, young Dick Juby carried off like an ape on the back of an adult clown mimicking a dog would have provoked more laughter among the Fortune's audience than the A-text's version of the episode. Casting a brilliant boy player as the second clown was a superb idea; it gave more opportunities for comic effect than in Q1, and a parody of the traditional, 'formulaic' actions performed by an adult player and a boy actor as dog and ape would have been more amusing to the audience than if they had been performed by two adults.

Casting Dick Juby in the revised *Faustus* might also have served to attract the audience's attention to the context of the so-called 'war of the theatres' between the adult acting companies and the children's companies; the Children of Paul's returned to the stage in 1599–1600, while the Children of the Chapel resumed acting in 1600.[56] Marston's praise of the boy actors in *Jack Drum's Entertainment*, first performed by Paul's Children in 1600, runs as follows: 'I sawe the Children of *Powles* last night, | And troth they pleasde mee prettie, prettie well, | The Apes [= mimics] in time will do it handsomely' (1601; STC 7243, sig. H3ᵛ). In line with such high esteem of boy actors, the company employed many of them: ten in *Frederick*, nine in *Tamar Cham*, and eight in *Alcazar*.[57] The introduction in Q4 *Faustus* of a young and gifted boy player perhaps reflects part of Bird and Rowley's strategic aim to compete in the current theatrical rivalry and find favour with the audience.

The casting of yet another boy player is suggested in the B-text. In the opening speech of the cup-stealing scene, Dick informs Robin that 'the Vintners boy followes vs at the hard heeles' (TLN 1140–1). The character who immediately enters pursuing them is 'Vintner' (1145). Since the 'Vintner' has invariably been identified by modern editors as an adult innkeeper selling wine, the inconsistency between the boy and the vintner has usually been ignored or it has been dismissed as the result of textual corruption.[58] But the possibility that 'Vintner' indicates the 'Vintners boy' cannot be completely ruled out. For example, in John Clavell's *The Soddered [Soldered] Citizen* (c. 1628–31), a transcribed playhouse manuscript, a '*Drawer*' (TLN 1105), as designated by the speech-prefix, enters to speak after the stage direction, '*Enter* […] *Vinteners Boyes*' (993).[59] The speech-prefix in a theatrical playbook (promptbook) is in

[55] Thomas Pettitt, 'Formulaic Dramaturgy in *Doctor Faustus*', in *'A Poet and a filthy Play-maker': New Essays on Christopher Marlowe*, ed. Kenneth Friedenreich, Roma Gill, and Constance B. Kuriyama (New York, 1988), 167–91, pp. 178–80.

[56] Chambers, *Elizabethan Stage*, 2.19–20, 41–2.

[57] Foakes, *Henslowe's Diary*, pp. 328–33. Only two are known in the fragmentary *Tennis*.

[58] Bevington and Rasmussen briefly comment on the textual inconsistency in *Doctor Faustus: A- and B-Texts*, pp. 167–8, 245 (commentary).

[59] *The Soddered Citizen*, ed. J. H. P. Pafford and W. W. Greg, Malone Society Reprints, 80 (Oxford, 1936), pp. 42, 47. For the date of the play, see Martin Wiggins with Catherine Richardson, *British Drama 1533–1642: A Catalogue: Volume VIII: 1624–1631* (Oxford, 2017), p. 468.

itself the sign of a speaker, not for the reader, but for actors and the bookkeeper. It was, therefore, sufficient that they would know precisely who would speak next, regardless of the verbal difference between 'Vintners boy' and 'Vintner'. The use of 'boy' in reference to adult male servants is attested by *OED* (*n.*[1] 1a) from about 1300, so it cannot be finally determined whether the 'Vintners boy' was played by an adult or a boy. But in the A-text, after '*enter the Vintner.*', Rafe speaks, 'But Robin, here comes the vintner.' (Q1, TLN 999–1000); his speech clearly indicates that the vintner in the A-text was an adult innkeeper. The deliberate alteration of 'the vintner' to 'the Vintners boy' in the B-text implies Bird and Rowley's intention to employ yet another boy actor in their revised comic scene.

It is plausible that, as sharers of the Admiral's/Nottingham's Men, Bird and Rowley were partly responsible not only for the revival of *Faustus*, but for keeping the company flourishing with Alleyn's successful return. During the five years' hiatus in performances of the play (there is no evidence that it was played after 1597) there would have been changes to the company's personnel, caused periodically by sickness, death, and retirement. Under the circumstances, sharers responsible for the management of the company would have had a sharp eye individually or collectively for their players' 'particular brilliance and appeal to audiences' and for 'where their own skills and those of their colleagues might appear to the best advantage'.[60] Young though he was, Dick Juby was probably a rising star, the most eminent and skilful of all boy players of Nottingham's Men around the turn of the century. It might have been natural, then, for Bird and Rowley to write parts of the comic scenes with Dick Juby in mind and to give his first name to the renamed second clown in their expanded *Faustus*.

From this discussion, it seems likely that Q4 contains the 'adicyones' commissioned by Henslowe from Bird and Rowley in 1602. Greg reported that the number of the B-text only lines was 679, accounting for a little less than a third of the entire text.[61] Eric Rasmussen listed the following seven passages as additions: (1) the rescue of Bruno passage (TLN 868–1083); (2) the 'Frederick/Martino/Benvolio' episode (1192–243); (3) Benvolio's revenge and Faustus's retaliation (1382–533); (4) the Clowns' tavern passages (1588–647, 1686–784); (5) Lucifer/Beelzebub against Faustus (1905–30); (6) Good/Bad Angels and their visions of heaven and hell (2006–45); and (7) the Scholars' discovery of Faustus's corpse (2104–32).[62] Of these passages, Greg identified Rowley as the probable author of addition (1), based on the use mostly at the end of verse lines of polysyllabic adjectives ending in '-all', an effect that can be observed in both his *When You See Me, You Know Me* (1605; STC 21417) and in Q4. In *When You See Me*, we find 'pompe pontificiall' (TLN 82), 'blessing Appostolicall' (833), 'pompe imperiall' (1435), 'Deitie supernall'

[60] John H. Astington, *Actors and Acting in Shakespeare's Time: The Art of Stage Playing* (Cambridge, 2010), p. 9.
[61] Greg, *Parallel Texts*, p. 74. Eric Rasmussen's count is 'some 676 lines', in his *A Textual Companion to 'Doctor Faustus'* (Manchester, 1993), p. 40.
[62] Rasmussen, *Textual Companion*, p. 41.

(2051), and 'treason Cappitall' (in the middle of 2653), while in Q4 addition (1) there are 'State Pontificall' (TLN 909), 'Statutes Decretall' (923 and in the middle of 1003), 'authority Apostolicall' (964), and 'blessing Apostolicall' (1015).[63] Identification of Bird's contributions appears almost impossible, for he left no single-authored play, but only a brief undated letter to Edward Alleyn.[64]

Bird and Rowley revised the entire text to produce not only the play's distinctive structure, but numerous minute verbal differences from the A-text. According to Fredson Bowers, the heavily revised passages include the comic episode between Robin and Dick (TLN 754–87, 1138–91), the German emperor and Bruno scene (1192–381), and the Old Man's speech (1823–40).[65] The B-text shows theatrical influence as well. The direction 'Exeunt.' appears twice at TLN 1137: once set at the end of the centred stage direction, and again on its far right on the same line. The location of the second 'Exeunt.' is similar to what bookkeepers often wrote in the right-hand margin of theatrical manuscripts to call attention to coming action. Paul Werstine, who examined the twenty-one surviving manuscript plays and all existing annotated printed texts, states that the repetition and transfer of the stage direction to the blank margin is a unique feature that cannot be observed elsewhere. The presence of what Werstine calls the 'notes for production' for the bookkeeper suggests that the B-text may indicate the influence of theatrical origin.[66]

There were other causes for variations in readings between the A- and the B-texts. Passages common to both texts show that, in accordance with the 1606 'Act to Restrain Abuses of Players', references to 'God' in Q1 were excised and altered to less offensive expressions in Q4; 'If vnto God' (Q1; TLN 529)/'If vnto heauen' (Q4; 477), 'Oh God, if' (Q1; 1493)/'O, if' (Q4; 2078), 'My God, my God' (Q1; 1515)/'O mercy heauen' (Q4; 2100), and 'What God' (Q1; 475)/'What power' (Q4; 424). Although in Q4 'O my God' (1962), 'O God forbid' (1969), and others still remained untouched, it is clear that the deletion of objectionable oaths was at least partially carried out to comply with current censorship. In view of the fact that the 1606 Act was in itself aimed at stage performance, it seems natural to connect the partly censored B-text with post-1606 performances. Further textual complications arise, because the B-text was obviously influenced by Q3 (1611). For instance, Q1's

[63] Greg, *Parallel Texts*, pp. 133–4. References to Rowley's play are to *When You See Me, You Know Me by Samuel Rowley 1605*, ed. F. P. Wilson, Malone Society Reprints, 97 (Oxford, 1952). Elsewhere in Q4 there are also 'demonstrations Magicall' (TLN 183) and 'state Maiesticall' (1277).
[64] See W. W. Greg, *Henslowe Papers* (London, 1907; repr. New York, 1975), pp. 85–6. A transcript of it can also be seen in 'The Fortune Theatre Records' (http://ereed.cch.kcl.ac.uk/home/), accessed 31 August 2017.
[65] *The Complete Works of Christopher Marlowe*, ed. Fredson Bowers, 2 vols (Cambridge, 1973), 2.134–5. According to the scene divisions outlined in n.8 above, the comic episode (TLN 754–87, 1138–91) and the German emperor and Bruno scene (1192–381) correspond to Scenes 7, 9, and 10, respectively.
[66] Paul Werstine, *Early Modern Playhouse Manuscripts and the Editing of Shakespeare* (Cambridge, 2012), pp. 239–41. See also Rasmussen, *Textual Companion*, p. 51.

'Oncaymæon' (Q1, TLN 52) reads 'Oeconomy' in both Q3 and Q4 (TLN 52), and Q1's 'Consissylogismes' (Q1, 155) is 'subtile sylogismes' in Q3 and 'subtle Sillogismes' in Q4 (145). In fact, Q4 adopted as many as 505 text-lines (by Greg's count) from its immediate predecessor.[67]

Q4 was transformed from Q1 (1604) by a range of additions, revisions, theatrical influences, post-1606 censorship, and adoption of Q3's text, as described above. It so happens that this textual transmission history perfectly fits E. K. Chambers's scepticism in his 1924 lecture, 'The Disintegration of Shakespeare', about the existence

> of the long-lived manuscript in the tiring-house wardrobe, periodically taken out for a revival and as often worked upon by fresh hands, abridged and expanded, recast to fit the capabilities of new performers, brightened with current topical allusions, written up to date to new tastes in poetic diction.

With his scathing criticism of this notion as disintegrative of the play text, Chambers went on to say, again sceptically, that 'Additional scenes may be inserted. If the old pages will no longer hold the new matter, they may be mutilated and replaced by partial transcripts'.[68] This concept of 'continuous copy' makes it extremely difficult to know not only the precise origin of the printer's copy and the exact transmission process it went through, but exactly which agents were involved in it up to its completion. The natural inference would be that the underlying manuscript of the multi-layered B-text could never have been suitable for the printer's use without passing through the intermediate stages of transcription. Somewhere in that process errors were inevitably introduced, such as the misplaced transfer of the comic scene (Scene 7; TLN 754–87) as well as the duplication of choruses (Chorus 2; 568–79 and Chorus 3; 788–812), as mentioned above. In these circumstances, it is hard to posit, as Greg did, that the printer's copy still contained Marlowe's foul papers more than a quarter of a century after the play was first composed.[69] Bowers concluded, *contra* Greg, that the printer's copy was 'a fresh inscription that had been made up from an underlying manuscript by some person hired by Wright', who often consulted Q3 as his main authority where necessary.[70] Rasmussen followed his lead in arguing that 'Wright had access to a composite manuscript that contained all of the latest revisions and additions', and that Wright made a transcript of it by 'concurrent transcription and collation' between the unwieldly composite manuscript and Q3. Okes's compositors were presumably supplied with the newly transcribed copy of what Rasmussen calls the 'hybrid' dramatic manuscript.[71] Doubtless the neat transcript helped in the accurate casting-off essential for setting the text by formes.

[67] Greg, *Parallel Texts*, pp. 65, 72–4.
[68] E. K. Chambers, 'The Disintegration of Shakespeare', in *Aspects of Shakespeare: Being British Academy Lectures* (Oxford, 1933), p. 42.
[69] Greg, *Parallel Texts*, p. 85.
[70] Bowers, *Complete Works*, 2.128.
[71] Rasmussen, *Textual Companion*, p. 54.

In the early decades of the seventeenth century, both the fame and notoriety of Faustus and his magical power seem to have been widespread in contemporary literature.[72] In *The Devil's Charter* (1607; STC 1466–6a), Barnabe Barnes borrowed two specific features from Marlowe's *Faustus*: the Pope is advised not to cross himself, and the main character wishes that his soul be dissolved rather than suffer eternal punishment.[73] Dekker referred to the 'wilde fire [that] flew from one to another, like squibs when Doctor *Faustus* goes to the diuell' in his *Work for Armourers* (1609; STC 6536), sig. F4[r]. On the Continent, the Archduchess Maria Magdalena, eighteen years old in 1608, wrote to her brother about the court festivities in Graz, the capital of Styria (now Steiermark, an Austrian state). An English troupe led by John Green performed ten plays there in February.[74] The Archduchess reported that 'Doctor Faustus' was performed on 10 February 1608.[75] Orlene Murad infers that either a copy of Q1 (1604) or the theatrical playbook of its earlier performances may have been available to Green.[76] The B-text performance at the Fortune in about 1620 is vividly described by John Melton's *Astrologaster* (1620; STC 17804, entered in the Stationers' Registers on 8 April 1620), in which the author recalls that 'shagge-hayr'd Deuills [that] runne roaring ouer the Stage with Squibs in their mouthes, while Drummers make Thunder in the Tyring-house, and the twelue-penny Hirelings make artificiall Lightning in their Heauens' (sig. E4[r]). In a comedy entitled *The Two Merry Milk-Maids* by 'J. C.' (1620; STC 4281), Julia asks, with imperfect memory, 'VVhy, haue we it not recorded, *Faustus* did | Fetch *Bruno*'s Wife, Duchesse of *Saxonie*, | In the dead time of Winter, Grapes she long'd for?' (sig. G1[r]; '*Bruno*' and '*Saxonie*' are in error). On the Continent again, the play was acted in Dresden on 7 July 1626 by the English troupe led by John Green.[77] Ben Jonson referred to the magician in *A Tale of a Tub* (1640; entered on 7 May 1633). In Act 4, Scene 6, Ball Puppy screams that 'I ha' seene the Divell | Among the straw: O for a Crosse ! a Collop | Of Friar *Bacon*, or a conjuring stick | Of Doctor *Faustus* ! Spirits are in the barne.' (sig. O4[r]).[78] In John Tatham's comedy, *Knavery in All Trades* (1664; Wing T220), there is an anecdote that an unnamed actor of Prince Charles's Men played 'the devil in Doctor F*austus*' (sig. E1[r]) at the

---

[72] For contemporary references to 'Faustus' and the records of the play's performance from the late 1580s up to 1597, see Hanabusa, *Doctor Faustus 1604*, pp. xxv–xxix.

[73] '*The Devil's Charter*' by Barnabe Barnes: A Critical Edition, ed. Jim C. Pogue, Garland Renaissance Drama (New York, 1980), pp. 18–22; Q1 *Faustus* (TLN 909–16); Q4 (1112–17).

[74] John Green's former affiliation in London is not known, as he 'is heard of only on the Continent'. See Edwin Nungezer, *A Dictionary of Actors* (New Haven, CT, 1929), pp. 159–61.

[75] Orlene Murad, 'The "Theatre Letter" of Archduchess Maria Magdalena: A Report on the Activities of the English Comedians in Graz, Austria, in 1608', *Mosaic*, 10 (1977), 119–31, pp. 120–1, 130.

[76] Orlene Murad, *The English Comedians at the Habsburg Court in Graz 1607–1608* (Salzburg, 1978), p. 44.

[77] Chambers, *Elizabethan Stage*, 2.285–6, 3.423.

[78] *A Tale of a Tub* forms part of the second volume of *The Works of Ben Jonson* (1640 [i.e. 1641]; STC 14754–4a), in which its separate title-page dates it as 'M.DC.XL'. For the text in modern spelling, see *A Tale of a Tub*, ed. Peter Happé, *The Cambridge Edition of the Works of Ben Jonson*, ed. David Bevington, *et al.*, 7 vols (Cambridge, 2012), 6.634 (4.6.29–32).

Fortune in about 1640.[79] During his performance, a tobacco-pipe was thrown at him by 'a fellow in the Gallery' who was, one may imagine, frightened by his realistic action.

NICHOLAS OKES AND JOHN WRIGHT

Nicholas Okes was freed from his apprenticeship to Richard Field on 5 December 1603.[80] In 1607 Okes took over the printing-house that George and Lionel Snowdon once owned in order to start his business as printer and publisher.[81] His son, John Okes, would also be freed by patrimony as a printer in 1627, and from about 1635–7 Nicholas and his son started to share imprints and collaborate. Their partnership lasted until 1642, shortly before son and father died, in 1643 and 1645, respectively.[82] In the first half of his long career, from 1607 to 1621, Nicholas produced 367 *STC* items.[83] The numbers of items by five-year division are 115 (1607–11; on average 23 items per year), 157 (1612–16; 31.4 items), and 95 (1617–21; 19 items). In 1616 alone, his printing-house produced thirty items, including Q4 *Faustus*, making 1616 one of the busiest of his first fifteen years in the trade. In that year, he seems to have been all the busier for being involved in the trouble caused by the printing of the English translation of St Francis de Sales's *An Introduction to a Devout Life* (1616; STC 11319). This translation contained 'a number of Catholic doctrines not accepted by Protestantism'. As a result, Okes was forced to remove offensive theological materials by printing seventeen duodecimo cancel leaves for as many as 1,500 copies. His extra work included 'many thousands of extremely laborious and time-consuming manual operations with knife and glue-pot'.[84]

Okes specialized, mainly but not exclusively, in small, topical, ephemera, into which category fell works of popular literature, including satirical pamphlets,

---

[79] Gerald Eades Bentley, *The Jacobean and Caroline Stage: Dramatic Companies and Players*, 7 vols (Oxford, 1941–68), 1.318–19.

[80] Arber, *Transcript*, 2.735. Okes originally apprenticed himself to William King, but was later transferred to Field. Field was the printer of the first four editions of Shakespeare's *Venus and Adonis* (1593–6; STC 22354–7) and the first edition of his *Lucrece* (1594; STC 22345).

[81] Jackson, *Records*, p. 24.

[82] Blayney, *Texts of 'King Lear'*, pp. 13–26, 292–313; *STC*, 3.129–30. ESTC conjectures that the date of Samuel Smith's *David's Repentance* (1640; STC 22846), Nicholas's final book, was 1642, not 1640 as on its title-page.

[83] The numbers here and below were produced by searching ESTC, accessed 25 December 2018.

[84] N. W. Bawcutt, 'A Crisis of Laudian Censorship: Nicholas and John Okes and the Publication of Sales's *An Introduction to a Devout Life* in 1637', *The Library*, 7th ser., 1 (2000), 403–38, p. 408.

jestbooks, epigrams, and so on.[85] For instance, he printed Dekker and George Wilkins's *Jests to Make You Merry* (1607; STC 6541) and Thomas Cooper's *The Mystery of Witchcraft* (1617; STC 5701). On the other hand, he issued, in the course of his career, more than seventy editions of contemporary plays, both outstanding and insignificant. The outstanding plays include, above all, the first editions of Shakespeare's *King Lear* (1608; STC 22292), *Othello* (1622; STC 22305), John Webster's *The White Devil* (1612; STC 25178), John Ford's *'Tis Pity She's a Whore* (1633; STC 11165), and Beaumont and Fletcher's Q1 and Q2 *Philaster* (1620, 1622; STC 1681–2). He also printed Shakespeare's *Lucrece* (1607; STC 22349) and Jonson's *The Masque of Queens* (1609; STC 14778). C. William Miller states that, except for William Wilson (active 1640–65), Okes effectively 'stands unchallenged [...] as the printer of items important in the history of English drama'.[86]

Peter W. M. Blayney argued that some of Okes's books 'are quite creditable pieces of work in the rather low-grade context of Jacobean London, but the majority are not', and that 'His average standard was good enough to allow him to compete for low-priced work, but was nevertheless poor'.[87] Antony Hammond and Doreen DelVecchio also criticized Okes, stating that he 'cannot be called a good printer, either in the technical or moral sense'.[88] Like many of his colleagues, Okes was never free from charges of disorderly printing: he was fined a number of times for unlicensed printing or for printing books whose rights were owned by other stationers.[89] He was also fined for keeping too many apprentices. In 1610, Okes took on two apprentices; a third joined him in June 1616, so that for the rest of the year in which Q4 was printed he had three apprentices, until one of them was freed in December.[90] This violated the Stationers' Company's rules, as Okes was technically allowed only to keep one apprentice.[91] Blayney states that 'if he could run his business on cheap apprentice labour, [Okes] was not particularly concerned whether or not the

[85] Paul A. Mulholland, 'Nicholas Okes', in *The British Literary Book Trade, 1475–1700*, ed. James K. Bracken and Joel Silver, *Dictionary of Literary Biography*, 170 (Detroit, MI, 1996), 193–8, pp. 193–4; 'Appendix B: Selected Stationer Profiles', in *Shakespeare's Stationers: Studies in Cultural Bibliography*, ed. Marta Straznicky (Philadelphia, PA, 2013), pp. 274–6.

[86] C. William Miller, 'A London Ornament Stock: 1598–1683', *Studies in Bibliography*, 7 (1955), 125–51, p. 129. William Wilson printed plays by Beaumont and Fletcher, William Davenant, James Shirley, and Abraham Cowley, among others.

[87] Blayney, *Texts of 'King Lear'*, p. 29.

[88] *The White Devil*, ed. Antony Hammond and Doreen DelVecchio, in *The Works of John Webster: An Old-Spelling Critical Edition*, ed. David Gunby, *et al.*, 3 vols (Cambridge, 1995–2007), 1.121.

[89] Jackson, *Records*, pp. 111, 135, 171, 443–4, 463, 467, 471–2, 475.

[90] By June 1616, Okes was keeping Abraham Fitzwaters and Benjamin Grendon. On 24 June, Andrew Driver's term of binding started, while Grendon's term ended on 2 December. See D. F. McKenzie, *Stationers' Company Apprentices 1605–1640* (Charlottesville, VA, 1961), p. 24.

[91] For this offence, no record of a fine exists. In 1610, he paid a fine of three shillings for a similar charge; see Jackson, *Records*, p. 444. The regulation originates from the 1586 Star Chamber Decree, by which up to two apprentices were exceptionally allowed for Under Wardens of the Company and up to three for Upper Wardens or Masters; see Arber, *Transcript*, 2.812.

apprentices were properly bound'.[92] Okes's defective standards as a craftsman were also recorded. In December 1625, he was censured by one Morgan for taking as many as five years to print merely six sheets of a book called *Speculum Animæ*. Okes was ordered by the Company to finish printing the remainder of the work (of which Morgan may have been the author) before the following Easter term, but the book was apparently never published.[93]

On the other hand, Okes's contemporary Thomas Heywood gave him the highest approval in 'To my approued good Friend, Mr *Nicholas Okes*.', at the end of his *An Apology for Actors* (1612; STC 13309) printed and published by Okes. Heywood praised Okes as 'so carefull, and industrious, so serious and laborious to doe the Author all the rights of the press', and concluded by remarking that 'I could wish but to bee the happy Author of so worthy a worke as I could willingly commit to your care and workmanship.' (sig. G4[r–v]). As the author of a work printed by Okes, his comments may smack of flattery; before 1612, part of Heywood's *The Rape of Lucrece* (1608; STC 13360) and *The Golden Age* (1611; STC 13325) had also been printed by him.[94] It still remains exceptional for an author to commend a printer in this way. The sincerity of Heywood's praise of Okes's skills in the craft is vindicated by the fact that, by 1615, five more titles of Heywood's were printed by Okes.[95] Inexperienced though his workmanship may have been in his early career, especially in 1607–8 when he printed Q1 *Lear* as his first play-quarto, it is also true that, four years before he set about the printing of Q4 *Faustus*, Okes (or his printing-house as a whole) could attain an adequate level of workmanship that would satisfy one of his profitable authors to such an extent. Heywood's praise, however, did not last for long; many troubles and disputes relating to his printing business followed immediately after it. Okes is conjectured to have been accused by Jonson, perhaps in 1623, as one of two 'ragged rascalls' (A4[r]) in his *Time Vindicated to Himself and to His Honours* ([1623]; STC 14782.5).[96] As has already been indicated, Okes was not a highly respectable member of the Stationers' Company, and, referring to his skills in printing, Blayney remarks that 'There were printers whose worst was worse than Okes's—but not very many, and not *much* worse'. Nonetheless, 'he can in several ways be considered usefully representative of the printers responsible for many […] important pre-Restoration play-quartos'.[97] Q4 *Faustus* can now be added to these.

[92] Blayney, *Texts of 'King Lear'*, p. 28.
[93] Jackson, *Records*, p. 180; Blayney, *Texts of 'King Lear'*, pp. 301–2.
[94] For the attribution of the printing of quires C–F of *The Rape of Lucrece* to Okes, see Peter W. M. Blayney, 'Quadrat Demonstrandum', *Papers of the Bibliographical Society of America*, 111 (2017), 61–101, p. 73 n.18.
[95] These are *The Brazen Age* (1613; STC 13310–0.3), *The Silver Age* (1613; STC 13365), *A Marriage Triumph* (1613; STC 13355), *The Four Prentices of London* (1615; STC 13321), and with Cyril Tourneur and John Webster, *Three Elegies* (1613; STC 24151).
[96] Blayney, *Texts of 'King Lear'*, pp. 300–1; but see *Time Vindicated to Himself and to his Honours*, ed. Martin Butler, in Bevington, *et al.*, *The Cambridge Edition of the Works of Ben Jonson*, 5.625, where the identification does not agree with Blayney's.
[97] Blayney, *Texts of 'King Lear'*, pp. 29, 292, respectively.

John Wright was apprenticed to his master Edward White from 1594 to 1602.[98] White 'dealt largely in ballads' as a bookseller, but he can also be deemed a renowned publisher of major Renaissance plays.[99] Wright started his independent career as a bookseller in 1605, became one of the Ballad Partners from 1624, and continued in the trade until a few years before his death in 1646.[100] Wright's will was proved on 21 March 1646.[101] His rights of ownership, including that of 'ye life & death of Doctor ffaustus, a play', were transferred to his younger brother Edward on 6 April 1646 (this was recorded on 27 June 1646).[102]

From the beginning of his career Wright published playbooks. In the first three years, from 1605 to 1607, five plays in six editions were issued by him. His first publication of a play-quarto was the only known edition of Q1 *King Leir* (1605; STC 15343) printed by Simon Stafford, who assigned the ownership of the play to Wright on condition that he print it.[103] In 1606–7, George Eld printed four plays for Wright, including Barnes's Q1 *The Devil's Charter*.[104] Soon afterwards, Wright's interest in play-publishing appears to have declined; he produced no more than a single play per year for the period between 1608 and 1615, during which time Q2–Q3 *Faustus* (1609, 1611) and Dekker's Q2 *The Shoemakers' Holiday* (1610; STC 6524) were printed for him by Eld. In 1609, Wright sold copies of *Shakespeare's Sonnets* (1609; STC 22353a) that Eld printed for Thomas Thorpe, and in the following year Wright secured the ownership rights to *Faustus* (as mentioned above) and *The Shoemakers' Holiday* through assignment from Bushell and Simmes, respectively.[105] The price of a bound (or unbound) copy of Q4 *Faustus* at Wright's bookshop is not known.[106]

---

[98] Arber, *Transcript*, 2.194, 732.

[99] *A Dictionary of Printers and Booksellers in England, Scotland and Ireland, and of Foreign Printers of English Books 1557–1640*, ed. Ronald B. McKerrow (London, 1910; repr. 1992), p. 288. White published the first editions of *Arden of Faversham* (1592; STC 733), *Soliman and Perseda* ([1592?]; STC 22894), Thomas Kyd's *The Spanish Tragedy* ([1592]; STC 15086), Shakespeare and George Peele's *Titus Andronicus* (1594; STC 22328), and Robert Greene's *Friar Bacon and Friar Bungay* (1594; STC 12267).

[100] *STC*, 3.190. Wright was also a 'bookebinder' in 1627; see William E. Miller, 'Printers and Stationers in the Parish of St. Giles Cripplegate 1561–1640', *Studies in Bibliography*, 19 (1966), 15–38, p. 38.

[101] Cyprian Blagden, 'Notes on the Ballad Market in the Second Half of the Seventeenth Century', *Studies in Bibliography*, 6 (1954), 161–80, p. 179.

[102] Greg, *Bibliography*, 1.55.

[103] Having been entered by Stafford on 8 May 1605, the play was assigned by him to Wright on the same day (Greg, *Bibliography*, 1.337).

[104] The remaining three plays are *The Second Part of the Return from Parnassus* (1606; STC 19309–10), *The Tragedy of Caesar and Pompey* ([1606?], 1607; STC 4339–40 [reissue with cancel title-page]), and John Day's *The Travails of the Three English Brothers* (1607; STC 6417).

[105] Greg, *Bibliography*, 1.26.

[106] Soon after their publication in 1594–5, an unbound copy of Marlowe's Q1 *Edward II* (1594; STC 17437) in twelve sheets was priced at six pence, while that of Shakespeare's O1 *The Third Part of Henry VI* (1595; STC 21006) in five sheets was sold at eight pence 'apparently in greater demand'; see Francis R. Johnson, 'Notes on English Retail Book-prices, 1550–1640', *The Library*, 5th ser., 5 (1950), 83–112, pp. 91, 106, 109.

The connection between Wright and Okes started in 1612 with the publication of Dekker's civic pageant, Q1 *Troia Nova Triumphans* (1612; STC 6530). It was maintained in 1615–16 as reflected in the publication of two more plays, Heywood's heroical romance, Q1 *The Four Prentices of London* (1615; STC 13321) that Okes printed for Wright, and Q4 *Faustus*. To enhance the books' visual appeal to potential buyers, presumably Wright, as the publisher of the two plays, decided to decorate each of their title-pages with a large woodcut; in Q1 *Four Prentices* four knights holding pikes are displayed. Q1 *Four Prentices* and Thomas Kyd's Q7 *The Spanish Tragedy*, also printed in 1615 (STC 15091–1a; printed by William White and sold by John White and Thomas Langley), were two of the first playbooks whose title-pages were illustrated with a woodcut describing 'the "scenic" convention of several figures engaged in action'.[107] Okes later reprinted Q2 *Four Prentices* (1632; STC 13322), on the title-page of which Okes decided, as the publisher this time, to reuse the same woodcut as in 1615.[108] Wright owned the woodcut of 'Faustus and Mephistopheles' for a long time and kept using it in the subsequent editions, as mentioned above. Later on, Wright and Okes collaborated in publishing the 'sixth Impression' of Arthur Dent's *A Sermon of God's Providence* (1616; STC 6649) and Thomas Cooper's pamphlet about murders, *The Cry and Revenge of Blood* (1620; STC 5698). In 1630, Okes assigned five religious books and pamphlets to Wright.[109]

Only a couple of years after he published Q4 *Faustus*, Wright's play-publishing strategy started to shift radically. In the twenty-two years from 1618 to 1639, he issued eighteen dramatic quartos, seventeen of which, surprisingly, comprise only three titles. He sporadically published Q5–Q9 *Faustus*, as mentioned above, Q7–Q15 *Mucedorus* ([1615–18, not in *STC* or ESTC], 1618, 1619, 1621, 1626, [1629?], 1631, 1634, 1639; STC 18236–41),[110] and Q3–Q5 *The Shoemakers' Holiday* (1618, 1624, 1631; STC 6525–7). It is worth noting that he acquired all three titles by assignment from his fellow stationers. These seventeen editions aside, the publication of Q2 *Fair Em* (1631; STC 7676), whose first edition had been published, probably in 1591, without entrance, is

[107] John H. Astington, *Stage and Picture in the English Renaissance: The Mirror up to Nature* (Cambridge, 2017), p. 183. Astington adds that 'all preceding illustrated title pages to plays […], from *If You Know Not Me* onwards, had displayed a single representative figure' (pp. 183–4). Queen Elizabeth is represented on the title-page of Heywood's Q1 *The First Part of If You Know Not Me, You Know Nobody* (1605; STC 13328, printed [by Thomas Purfoot] for Nathaniel Butter).

[108] The title-page imprint of Q2 *Four Prentices* states that it was 'Printed at *London* by *Nicholas Okes*. 1632.', despite the fact that the rights of ownership of the play had been assigned from him to his son on 2 August 1630 (Greg, *Bibliography*, 1.38). The visual effect of the famous woodcut in *The Spanish Tragedy* was also sufficient for it to be reused in all later reprints Q8–Q10 (1618, 1623, 1633; STC 15092–4).

[109] Arber, *Transcript*, 4.238–9.

[110] *Mucedorus* was assigned to Wright on 17 September 1618 (Greg, *Bibliography*, 1.31). The date of the '1615–18' edition, only five leaves of which survive, has been conjectured by Richard Proudfoot, in '"Modernizing" the Printed Play-Text in Jacobean London: Some Early Reprints of *Mucedorus*', in *'A Certain Text': Close Readings and Textual Studies on Shakespeare and Others in Honor of Thomas Clayton*, ed. Linda Anderson and Janis Lull (Newark, NJ, 2002), pp. 18–28.

exceptional. Since it was never republished thereafter, as all the three assigned plays were, it is possible to conjecture that Q2 did not bring a large profit to Wright, contrary to his original expectations.

Wright tended to select profitable plays from among the editions already circulating in the book market. He published reprints of plays assigned to him in order to save the initial outlay on a payment to the author or to the dramatic company that owned the play script, or to a scribe if a transcription was necessary. Wright was a bookseller who eagerly collected assigned titles; it is remarkable that approximately 190 titles (including part-assignments) were transferred to him between 1605 and 1638. To mention only a few, *The History of Doctor Faustus*, the prose version of the Faust Book, was assigned to him in 1619, 1620, and 1634; *Venus and Adonis* was transferred in 1626 and was re-entered in 1638; and, remarkably, Marlowe's *Edward II* was assigned to Wright and John Haviland jointly in 1638, but no reprint of the play seems to have followed.[111] In view of the limited number of play titles in Wright's output from 1618, as well as his strictly conservative and cost-saving trading practices, it is likely that sometime after he issued Q4 *Faustus* he determined to reduce his play-publishing activities and to find a new market for a different product, ballads. In the latter half of his career, Wright trod a similar path to that of his master, Edward White. From 1624, Wright, together with Henry Gosson, to whom he would lease the 'Faust and Mephistopheles' woodcut in 1628,[112] became a member of the Ballad Partners, the six members of the Stationers' Company who maintained a common stock of ballads.[113] Ballads that did not just have a topical appeal, but that exhibited romantic, adventurous, or supernatural characteristics, formed a profitable market.[114] To publish such saleable ballads alone or jointly and to guard their rights of ownership, the Ballad Partners entered, on 11 December 1624, 128 ballads en bloc, consisting largely of old Elizabethan stock, of which the ballad version of Faustus was one.[115] With this, Wright became de facto the exclusive copy-holder of all three versions: the play, the prose narrative, and the ballad (part-copy) of the 'Faustus Legend'.

[111] See Jackson, *Records*, pp. 112–13 and Arber, *Transcript*, 4.44, 318; 4.160, 431; 4.434. For the key to finding his assigned titles, see Arber, *Transcript*, 5.cxi. It should be noted that some 115 titles, including *Greene's Groatsworth of Wit* (1592, 1596, 1617, 1621, 1629; STC 12245–9), *The Wisdom of Doctor Dodypoll* (1600; STC 6991), and Marston's *Parasitaster or the Fawn* (1606, 1633; STC 17472, 17483–4), were assigned jointly to Wright and John Haviland in 1638 alone (Arber, *Transcript*, 4.431–4).

[112] See above, p. x, n.6.

[113] The six stationers were Thomas Pavier, John Wright, his brothers Cuthbert and Edward Wright, John Grismond, and Henry Gosson; see Blagden, 'Notes on the Ballad Market', p. 165.

[114] Blagden, 'Notes on the Ballad Market', pp. 161–3.

[115] Arber, *Transcript*, 4.131–2.

The unique copy of Q4 is one of approximately 1,300 plays formerly owned by David Garrick (1717–79), actor, theatre manager, and dramatist.[116] In his will, Garrick stipulated that 'I Give and bequeath […] all my Collection of old English Plays to the Trustees of the British Museum for the time being for the Use of the Publick'.[117] The Garrick Collection reached the British Museum in April 1780. Apart from the bound volumes in the George Thomason Tracts, Garrick's plays were almost the only plays in the Museum until the arrival of the King's Library in 1828. The Garrick Collection comprised both single and collected volumes of plays published between 1510 and 1720, being richest in those of the late sixteenth and the seventeenth centuries. From Robert Dodsley (1704–64), the publisher of twelve volumes of *A Select Collection of Old Plays* (1744–6), Garrick purchased more than 550 plays that Dodsley had obtained from Edward Harley (1689–1741), second Earl of Oxford.[118] As soon as Garrick's plays were received, the Museum stamp was impressed in yellow on the verso of Q4's title-page (sig. A1ᵛ), as well as between the Latin motto and 'F I N I S.' on H3ᵛ (TLN 2133–4), signifying that it was a gift.[119] The Garrick Collection also includes a single copy each of Q7 and Q9 *Faustus*.[120]

Shortly before 1756, Garrick engaged Edward Capell (1713–81) to draw up a catalogue of his collection.[121] Capell's manuscript inventory (now held in the British Library), 'A Catalogue of Plays; the Collection of David Garrick, Esq;',[122] lists Q4 *Faustus* as '[No.] 460. Doctor Faustus. H[istory]. 4°. Ch. Mar. 1616. f[or]. John Wright. K.XV.'; in accordance with Capell's scheme for the binding of the collection, 'K' indicates the bound volume's size, and 'XV' refers to the volume's place within the sequence of volumes of that size. In a footnote, Marlowe's full name, 'Christopher Marloe', as well as 'Lang.', the abbreviated name of Gerard Langbaine, the author of *The Lives and Characters of the English Dramatic Poets* (1699), are supplied in Capell's hand.[123] In

---

[116] For Garrick's Collection, see George M. Kahrl with Dorothy Anderson, *The Garrick Collection of Old English Plays: A Catalogue with an Historical Introduction* (London, 1982) and Nicholas D. Smith, *An Actor's Library: David Garrick, Book Collecting and Literary Friendships* (New Castle, DE, 2017). I am grateful to Tanya Kirk, Lead Curator of the British Library, for providing information on Garrick and his library.

[117] Smith, *An Actor's Library*, p. 207.

[118] George Winchester Stone, Jr and George M. Kahrl, *David Garrick: A Critical Biography* (Carbondale, IL, 1979), pp. 169–70.

[119] Kahrl with Anderson, *The Garrick Collection of Old English Plays*, p. 50.

[120] The Collection also holds Marlowe's Q2–Q4 *Edward II* (1598, 1612, 1622; STC 17438, 17439.5, 17440, 17440a), Q1 *The Jew of Malta* (1633; STC 17412), Q1 *The Massacre at Paris* ([1594?]; STC 17423), and O2 and O4 *The First and Second Parts of Tamburlaine* (1593, 1605–6; STC 17426, 17428, 17428a); these copies are described with Q4 *Faustus* in Kahrl with Anderson, *The Garrick Collection of Old English Plays*, pp. 182–4.

[121] Stone, Jr and Kahrl, *David Garrick*, p. 175.

[122] Kahrl with Anderson, *The Garrick Collection of Old English Plays*, pp. 20–5, plates 1 and 2, facing pp. 64 and 65. Capell's catalogue in the BL is probably a later fair copy of the original; the Library conjectures that it was made in about 1778.

[123] Capell's 'Catalogue', p. 56. Rebacked in 1934, the catalogue currently consists of two bound volumes, with the shelfmark 643.l.30. The volumes have been digitized by the British Library.

1841–6, Garrick's volumes were broken up, and each play was separately rebound under the supervision of Antonio Panizzi, Keeper of Printed Books.[124] The copy of Q4 was rebound by Charles Tuckett, Sr, the Museum binder, in full red morocco with Garrick's coat of arms in gold.[125]

*

The present photographic facsimile comprises a 1:1 full-colour reproduction of the unique copy of Q4 in the British Library.

The inner margins provide 'Through Line Numbers', beginning with the title on sig. A1[r]. Catchwords are not included in the count.

---

[124] Kahrl with Anderson, *The Garrick Collection of Old English Plays*, pp. 64–7.

[125] 'TUCKETT. BINDER. BRITISH MUSEUM' is stamped in gilt on the turn-in on the back of the upper board. For Tuckett, Sr, see P. R. Harris, *A History of the British Museum Library 1753–1973* (London, 1998), p. 43. Garrick's coat of arms was reproduced in Dorothy Anderson, 'Reflections on Librarianship: Observations Arising from Examination of the Garrick Collection of Old Plays in the British Library', *British Library Journal*, 6.1 (Spring, 1980), 1–6, p. 5.

APPENDIX

LIST OF NICHOLAS OKES'S DAMAGED TYPES

The damaged types are listed alphabetically, with two majuscules followed by the single minuscule; the books in which the damaged types occur are arranged in order of the date of publication. The libraries holding the copies that were inspected are abbreviated as: C (Cambridge University Library), L (British Library), M (Meisei University Library, Tokyo), and O (Bodleian Library). The identified types are listed by signature, line numbers, and the word in which the specific type (printed here in bold face) was used.

Majuscule 'B'

E4^r/32 (TLN 1334) **B**envolio

1. Arthur Hopton, *A Concordancy of Years* (1616; STC 13780)
   Private owner
   K2^v/8 **B** A
2. Thomas Cooper, *The Mystery of Witchcraft* (1617; STC 5701)
   L (719.b.20), O (8° C 176 Th)
   Z6^r/25 **B**y
3. Samuel Daniel, *The Collection of the History of England* ([1618]; STC 6248)
   C (Peterborough.C.7.2), L (2 copies, C.175.dd.17 and 597.i.2), O (D 2.16 Art)
   K4^v/29 **B**ut; L6^v/29 **B**rittaine; M2^v/4 **B**arons; N3^r/1 **B**esides; O2^v/55 **B**ut

Majuscule 'M'

B2^r/17 (TLN 310) **M**eph.

1. Thomas Dekker, *The Honest Whore* (1615; STC 6503)
   L (644.b.19), M (MR 1169 [1616; STC 6504, an imprint variant of STC 6503])
   F1^v/11 **M**y; H3^r/30 **M**eet; I3^v/24 **M**oone
2. William Est, *The Right Rule of a Religious Life* (1616; STC 10536)
   L (1477.d.7), O (8° S 139 (2) Th)
   L5^v/26 **M**onarch
3. John Marston, *The Insatiate Countess* (1616; STC 17477)
   L (C.122.d.27), O (Mal.252 (9))
   D1^r/4 **M**ine; H4^v/6 **M**ight

Minuscule 'n'

E4^v/22 (TLN 1360) Argiro**n**, H1^v/26 (TLN 1993) Exeu**n**t

1. John Napier, *A Description of the Admirable Table of Logarithms* (1616; STC 18351)
L (C.112.a.12), O (Tanner 465 (1))
A5^v/2 **n**umbers
2. Thomas Playfere, *The Mean in Mourning* (1616; STC 20019)
C (Syn.8.61.111), L (4452.aaa.16.(1)), O (Vet.A2 f.276 (1))
L7^v/18 thi**n**gs; N2^r/15 opi**n**ion
3. Samuel Smith, *David's Blessed Man* (1616; STC 22839.5)
O (Vet.A2 f.275)
D3^v/9 blessed**n**esse; F2^v/16 a**n**d; I4^r/9 i**n**to; Y6^r/12 Dominio**n**
4. Thomas Cooper, *The Mystery of Witchcraft* (1617; STC 5701)
L (719.b.20), O (8° C 176 Th)
K8^r/25 Co**n**science
5. Samuel Daniel, *The Collection of the History of England* ([1618]; STC 6248)
C (Peterborough.C.7.2 [leaf C1 missing]), L (2 copies, C.175. dd.17 and 597.i.2), O (D 2.16 Art)
C1^v/45 ge**n**erall; K1^v/45 i**n**; P1^v/43 withi**n**; Q4^v/42 i**n**countred

'**B**envolio' (E4^r/32, TLN 1334)
(Reproduced by permission
of the British Library)

The Mystery of Witchcraft, 1617, Z6^r/25
(Reproduced by permission
of the Bodleian Library)

'**M**eph.' (B2^r/17, TLN 310)
(Reproduced by permission
of the British Library)

The Insatiate Countess, 1616, D1^r/4
(Reproduced by permission
of the Bodleian Library)

'Exe**u**nt' (H1^v/26, TLN 1993)
(Reproduced by permission
of the British Library)

David's Blessed Man, 1616, Y6^r/12
(Reproduced by permission
of the Bodleian Library)

LIST OF ROLES

(In order of their appearance in the 1616 quarto)

Chorus
Doctor Faustus, a scholar
Wagner, Faustus's servant
The Good Angel
The Bad Angel
Valdes, Faustus's friend
Cornelius, Faustus's friend
Two Scholars
Lucifer, the principal devil
Four Devils attending Lucifer
Mephistopheles, a devil
Robin, the clown
Banio, a devil
Belcher, a devil
A woman devil
Beelzebub, a devil, Lucifer's companion
Pride
Covetousness
Envy
Wrath
Gluttony
Sloth
Lechery
Dick, Robin's colleague
The Cardinal of France
The Cardinal of Padua
The Archbishop of Rheims
A Bishop
Monks, attending the Pope
Friars, attending the Pope
Pope Adrian
Lord Raymond, King of Hungary
Bruno of Saxony, the rival Pope
Attendants serving Pope Adrian's banquet
A Vintner
Martino, a knight attending the Emperor
Frederick, a knight attending the Emperor
Benvolio, a young man
Charles, the Emperor of Germany
Attendants on the Emperor
A Spirit representing Alexander the Great
A Spirit representing Darius
A Spirit representing Alexander's Paramour

Belimoth, a devil
Argiron, a devil
Ashtaroth, a devil
Soldiers, attending Benvolio
Military Devils
A Horse-Courser
A Carter
A Hostess
The Duke of Anhalt
The Duchess of Anhalt
A Servant
Devils serving a banquet
Three Scholars
A Spirit of Helen of Troy
An Old Man
Two Cupids

OBSCURED AND DAMAGED READINGS

The following list consists of readings containing broken, blotted, or uninked letters and punctuation; turned letters (mostly 'u' and 'n', but at TLN 569 'Faustus' with ²s turned and at 1223 with the interrogation mark turned) have not been recorded. Roman and black-letter readings are represented in roman. Each missing or unclear piece of type is represented by a point between angle brackets. In the case of TLN 4, Marlowe's abbreviated name has been altered and expanded by pen and ink; this has not been recorded here. In TLN 1251: 1288, 1469: 1502, 1536: 1571, 1605: 1642, 1675: 1708, and 2099: 2132, the reading has become obscured due to a crease in the paper. Signatures are illegible at lines 331+ (B2), 617+ (C2), 690+ (C3). Catchwords are illegible or missing as follows: 74+ (When), 148+ (On), 222+ (is), 331+ (To), 367+ (like), 439+ (Faust.), 475+ (Homo), 511+ (said), 582+ (Because), 617+ (Meph.), 655+ (Faust.), 728+ (mother), 765+ (Rob.), 801+ (Not), 949+ (And), 1022+ (A), 1056+ (Lord), 1094+ (Faust.), 1230+ (I), 1375+ (an), 1584+ (Faust.), 1720+ (Horse.), 1859+ (Reuolt,), 2004+ (Fooles), 2076 (O). Readings with an asterisk signal that they are wholly or in part not visible in this photographic facsimile edition, usually because they are obscured by the volume's gutter; they can, however, be seen in the 1970 Scolar Press facsimile edition of Q1 and Q4. The 'Full' readings have been verified against Greg's *Parallel Texts* and the Scolar Press facsimile.

TLN	Visible Reading	Full Reading
7	sig<..>	signe
8	Bibl<..>	Bible.
51	greate<.>	greater
52	O<..>onomy	Oeconomy
53	<....>itian	Phisitian
54	e<...>niz'd	eterniz'd
74+ (CW)	W<...>	When
105	<.>reater	greater
106	s<.> <...>t.	so fast.
*148+ (CW)	O<.>	On
156	B<.>	Be
157	Li<.>c	Like
*166	<.>f	If
*168	<.>s t<.>ou	As thou
*170	<.>i<..>	Will
*171	<.>e	He
*172	<.>n<...>ht	Inricht
*173	<.>ath	Hath
*174	<.>hen	Then
*175	<.>nd <.>ore	And more
*176	<.>he<.>	Then

*177	<.>he	The
*178	<.>nd	And
*179	<.>ea	Yea
*180	<.>ithin	Within
*181	<.>hen	Then
*183	<..>me	Come
*184	<.>hat	That
*185	<..>d	And
*213	²y<.>u	you
*214	question <.>	question:
*218	for<.>	for⸗
*219	bu<.>	but
*220	tri<.>	tri⸗
*221	Precisian<.>	Precisian,
*222	M<..>	M^r.
397	m<.>trally	metrally
*471	<.>ow	Now
*474	<.>nd	And
622	Who<.>e	Whose
*695	he<.> <.>ecke	her Necke
*696	<.>hen	then
*711	com<.>	come
*712	alon<..> <.>hen	alone, then
*713	and <.>	and I
728	god<.>	god⸗
733	Glu<..>	Glut.
*770	wh<...>	what,
*771	<....>es	hornes
*772	(it<.>	(it.
*806	w<.>th	with
842	Venso<..>	Venson.
881	<..>ow'st	know'st
*909	<.>aint	Saint
*911	<.>ut	But
917	woo<.>	wool
1026	<.>ow	Now
*1036	<..>	me
*1052	<.>est	Lest
*1071	charge<.>	charge.
*1194	<.>ye	Hye
*1195	<.>ood	Good
1288	diue<..> <.>ouernor	diuels Gouernor
1301	Il'<.>e	Il'e
*1331	<.>hrusts	thrusts
1344	ma<...>r	matter
*1525	<.>e'd	He'd

*1531	<.>ith	Sith
*1532	<.>e'le	We'le
*1537	<.>ollors	Dollors
*1539	<.>mall	small
*1540	<..>kest	likest
*1541	<.>ast	hast
*1543	<.>an	man
*1544	<.>argaine	bargaine
*1546	<.>ey	ney
*1547	<.>edge	hedge
*1548	<..>se	case
*1550	<.>f	of
1571	<.>or	for
	<.>urn<..> <.>o	turned to
1582	earne<...>	earnest⸗
1583	t<.>	to
*1590	<.>n	in
*1602	<.>o	no
1605	<.>o <...> <.>ill	do now till
*1606	<.>omes	comes
*1608	<.>urer	iurer
*1610	<.>o	to
*1614	<.>ould	could
*1615	<.>urne	turne
*1616	<.>o	so
*1617	<.>m	am
*1618	<.>y	my
*1630	bu<.>	but
*1631	mids<.>	midst
*1637	bu<.>	but
1642	<.>euils <.>urn'<.>	deuils turn'd
1654	A<.>	As
*1660	<.>ire	sire
*1661	<.>hat	that
*1662	<.>ainty	dainty
*1665	<.>aue	haue
*1666	<.>ime	time
*1667	<.> dish	a dish
*1670	<.>adam	Madam
*1672	<.>ere	Here
*1673	<.>or	For
*1675	<.>t	at
	eu<..>y T<..>e	euery Tree
*1676	<..>uite	fruite
*1678	<.>ircles	circles
*1679	<.>s	vs

*1680	<.>s	as
*1681	<.>here	where
*1682	<.>f	of
*1683	<.>ou	you
*1685	<..>re <.>	e're I
*1724	Faus<..>	Faust.
1751	nig<.>t	night
*1753	<.>est	kest
1755	<.> would	I would
1793	ther'<.>	ther's
*1799	<.>aire	faire
*1800	<.>aue	haue
*1801	<.>he	the
*1803	<.>ame	dame
*1804	<.>hould	should
*1807	<.>he	The
*1808	<.>ou	You
*1809	<.>o	No
*1810	<.>hen	Then
*1811	<.>nd	And
*1812	<.>e	Be
*1816	<.>ade	Made
*1818	<.>hom	Whom
*1820	<.>ee'l	Wee'l
*1821	<.>appy	Happy
*1841	don<..>	done?
*1842	giue<.>	giues
*1843	dag<.>	dag-
*1859+ (CW)	Reuolt<.>	Reuolt,
*1965	<.>ift	lift
2099	an<.> en<.>er <.>he	and enter the
2109	<.>ray	Pray
2132	th<.>n <.>eauen<.>y	then heauenly
2133	hor<.>	hora

The Tragicall History
of the Life and Death
of *Doctor Faustus.*

Written by *Ch. Marklin.*

LONDON,
Printed for *Iohn Wright,* and are to be fold at his fhop
Without Newgate, at the f... ..of the
Bib.. 1616.

1

THE
TRAGEDIE OF
Doctor Fauſtus.

Enter Chorus.

NOt marching in the fields of Thraſimen,
Where Mars did mate the warlicke Carthagens,
Nor ſporting in the dalliance of loue
In Courts of kings, where ſtate is ouer-turn'd
Nor in the pompe of proud audacious deeds,
Intends our Muſe to vaunt his heauenly verſe
Onely this, Gentles: we muſt now performe
The forme of Fauſtus fortunes, good or bad,
And now to patient iudgements we appeale,
And ſpeake for Fauſtus in his infancie.
Now is he borne, of parents baſe of ſtocks,
In Germany, within a Towne cal'd Rhodes.
At riper yeares to Wittenberg he went,
Whereas his kinſmen chiefly brought him vp;
So much he profits in Diuinitie,
That ſhortly he was grac'd with Doctors name,
Excelling all, and ſweetly can diſpute
In th'heauenly matters of Theologie,
Till ſwolne with cunning, of a ſelfe conceit,
His waxen wings did mount aboue his reach,
And melting, heauens conſpir'd his ouer-throw:
For falling to a diuelliſher erciſe,
And glutted now with learnings golden gifts,
He ſurfets vpon curſed Necromancie:

A 2   Nothing

3

Nothing so sweet as Magicke is to him;
Which he preferres before his chiefest blisse,
And this the man that in his study sits.

Faustus in his study.

Faust. Settle thy studies Faustus, and begin
To sound the depth of that thou wilt professe,
Hauing commenc'd, be a Diuine in shew,
Yet leuell at the end of euery Art,
And liue and die in Aristotles workes.
Sweet Analitikes, tis thou hast rauisht me,
Bene disserere est finis Logicis.
Is to dispute well Logickes chiefest end?
Affords this Art no greater miracle?
Then read no more, thou hast attain'd that end:
A greater subiect fitteth Faustus wit:
Bid Oeconomy farewell; and Galen come:
Be a _ _ sitian Faustus, heaps vp gold,
And be eterniz'd for some wondrous cure:
Summum bonum, medicinæ sanitas,
The end of Physicke is our bodies health:
Why Faustus, hast thou not attain'd that end?
Are not thy bils hung vp as monuments,
Wherby whole Cities haue escap't the plague,
And thousand desperate maladies beene cur'd?
Yet art thou still but Faustus, and a man.
Couldst thou make men to liue eternally,
Or being dead, raise them to life againe,
Then this profession were to be esteem'd.
Physicke farewell: where is Iustinian?
Si vna eademque res legatus duobus,
Alter rem, alter valorem rei, &c.
A petty case of paltry Legacies,
Exhereditari filium non potest pater, nisi——
Such is the subiect of the institute,
And vniuersall body of the law.
This study fits a Mercenarie drudge,
Who aimes at nothing but externall trash,
Too seruile and illiberall for mee.

When all is done, Diuinitie is best :
Ieromes Bible Faustus, view it well:
Stipendium peccati, mors est : ha, stipendium,&c.
The reward of sin is death? that's hard:
Si peccasse, negamus, fallimur, & nulla est in nobis veritas:
If we say that we haue no sinne
We deceiue our selues, and there is no truth in vs.
Why then belike we must sinne,
And so consequently die,
I, we must die, an euerlasting death.
What doctrine call you this? Che sera, sera:
What will be, shall be; Diuinitie adeiw.
These Metaphisicks of Magitians,
And Negromantick bookes are heauenly,
Lines,Circles,Letters,Characters :
I these are those that Faustus most desires.
O what a world of profite and delight,
Of power, of honour, and omnipotence,
Is promised to the Studious Artizan?
All things that moue betweene the quiet Poles
Shall be at my command : Emperors and kings,
Are but obey'd in their seuerall Prouinces :
But his dominion that exceeds in this,
Stretcheth as farre as doth the mind of man:
A sound Magitian is a Demi-god,   Enter Wagner.
Here tire my braines to get a Deity.
Wagner, commend me to my deerest friends,
The Germane Valdes and Cornelius,
Request them earnestly to visit me.
   Wag. I will sir.   Exit.
   Faust. Their conference will be a greater helpe to me,
Then all my labours, plod I ne're so fast.

Enter the Angell and Spirit.

   Good A. O Faustus, lay that damned booke aside,
And gaze not on it least it tempt thy soule,
And heape Gods heauy wrath vpon thy head.
Reade,

Reade, reade the Scriptures : that is blasphemy.

    Bad A. Go forward Fauſtus in that famous Art
Wherein all natures treaſure is contain'd :
Be thou on earth as Ioue is in the ſkye,
Lord and Commander of theſe elements :   Exeunt An.

    Fauſt. How am I glutted with conceipt of this?
Shall I make ſpirits fetch me what I pleaſe ?
Reſolue me of all ambiguities?
Performe what deſperate enterprize I will?
I'le haue them flie to Indian for gold;
Ranſacke the Ocean for Orient Pearle,
And ſearch all corners of the new-found-world
For pleaſant fruites, and Princely delicates.
I'le haue them read me ſtrange Philoſophy,
And tell the ſecrets of all forraine Kings:
I'le haue them wall all Germany with Braſſe,
And make ſwift Rhine, circle faire Wittenberge :
I'le haue them fill the publique Schooles with ſkill,
Wherewith the Students ſhall be brauely clad.
I'le leauy ſouldiers with the coyne they bring,
And chaſe the Prince of Parma from our Land,
And raigne ſole King of all the Prouinces.
Yea ſtranger engines for the brunt of warre,
Then was the fiery keele at Anwerpe bridge,
I'le make my ſeruile ſpirits to inuent.
Come Germane Valdes and Cornelius,
And make me bleſt with your ſage conference.   Enter Valdes
Valdes, ſweete Valdes and Cornelius,   and Cornelius.
Know that your words haue won me at the laſt.
To practiſe Magicke and concealed Arts.
Philoſophy is odious and obſcure :
Both Law and Phyſicke are for petty wits,
'Tis magick, magick, that hath rauiſht me.
Then gentle friends aid me in this attempt,
And I, that haue with ſubtle Sillogiſmes
Grauel'd the Paſtors of the Germane Church,
And made the floWring pride of Wittenberg
Sworne to my Problemes, as th'infernall ſpirits

On sweet Muſæus when he came to hell,
Will be as cunning as Agrippa was,
Whose ſhadow made all Europe honour him.

    Val. Fauſtus, theſe bookes, thy wit, and our experience,
ſhall make all Nations to Canonize vs,
As Indian Moores, obey their Spaniſh Lords:
So ſhall the ſpirits of euery element,
B alwaies ſeruiceable to vs three:
Like Lyons ſhall they guard vs when we pleaſe,
Like Almaine Rutters with their horſemens ſtaues,
Or Lopland Giants trotting by our ſides,
Sometimes like women or vnwedded Maides:
Shadowing more beauty in their Airie browes,
Then has the white breaſts of the Queene of loue.
From Venice ſhall they drag huge Argoſies,
And from America the Golden Fleece,
That yearely ſtuft old Phillips treaſury,
If learned Fauſtus will be reſolute.

    Fauſt. Valdes, as reſolute am I in this,
As thou to liue, therefore obiect it not.

    Corn. The miracles that magick will performe,
Will make thee vow to ſtudy nothing elſe.
He that is grounded in Aſtrology,
In ſeht with tongues, well ſeene in Minerals,
Hath all the Principles Magick doth require:
Then doubt not Fauſtus but to be renowm'd,
And more frequented for this myſterie,
Then heeretofore the Delphian Oracle.
The ſpirits tell me they can dry the ſea,
And fetch the treaſure of all forraine wracks:
Yea all the wealth that our fore-fathers hid,
Within the maſſy entrailes of the earth:
Then tell me Fauſtus what ſhall we three want?

    Fauſt. Nothing Cornelius; O this cheeres my ſoule:
Come, ſhew me ſome demonſtrations Magicall,
That I may coniure in ſome buſhy Groue,
And haue theſe ioies in full poſſeſſion.

    Val. Then haſt thee to ſome ſolitary Groue,

And

7

And beare wiſe Bacons, and Albanus woꝛkes,
The Hebrew Pſalter, and new Teſtament;
And whatſoeuer elſe is requiſite,
We will infoꝛme thee e're our conference ceaſe.

    Cor. Valdes, firſt let him know the woꝛds of Art,
And then all other ceremonies learn'd,
Fauſtus may try his cunning by himſelfe.

    Val. Firſt I'le inſtruct thee in the rudiments,
And then wilt thou be perfecter then I.

    Fauſt. Then come and dine with me, and after meate
We'le canuaſe euery quidditie thereof:
Foꝛ e're I ſleep, I'le try what I can do:
This night I'le coniure tho I die therefoꝛe.   Exeunt om.

Enter two Schollers.

    1 Sch. I wonder what's become of Fauſtus that was wont
To make our ſchooles ring, with ſic probo.   Enter Wag.

    2 Sch. That ſhall we pꝛeſently know, here comes his boy.

    1 Sch. How now ſirra, where's thy Maiſter?

    Wag. God in heauen knowes.

    2 Sch. Why doſt not thou know then!

    Wag. Yes, I know, but that followes not.

    1 Sch. Go to ſirra, leaue your ieſting, & tell vs where he is.

    Wag. That followes not by foꝛce of argument, which
you, being Licentiats, ſhould ſtand vpon, therefoꝛe acknow-
ledge your errour, and be attentiue.

    2 Sch. Then you will not tell vs?

    Wag. You are deceiu'd, foꝛ I will tell you: yet if you
were not dunces, you would neuer aſke me ſuch a queſtion:
Foꝛ is he not Corpus naturale? and is not that Mobile? Then
wherefoꝛe ſhould you aſke me ſuch a queſtion? But that I
am by nature flegmatique, ſlow to wꝛath, & pꝛone to letcherie
(to loue I would ſay) it were not foꝛ you to come within foꝛ-
tie foot of the place of execution, although I do not doubt but
to ſee you both hangd the next Seſſions. Thus hauing triumpht ouer you, I will ſet my countenance like a Pꝛeciſian
and begin to ſpeake thus: Truely my deere bꝛethꝛen, my M

is within at dinner, with Valdes and Cornelius, as this wine,
if it could ſpeake, would informe your Worſhips: and ſo
the Lord bleſſe you, preſerue you, and keepe you, my deere
brethren.   Exit.

    1 Sch. O Fauſtus, then I feare y which I haue long ſuſpected:
That thou art falne into that damned Art
For which they two are infamous through the world.
    2 Sch. Were he a ſtranger, not allyed to me,
The danger of his ſoule would make me mourne :
But come, let vs go, and informe the Rector :
It may be his graue counſell may reclaime him.
    1 Sch. I feare me, nothing will reclaime him now.
    2 Sch. Yet let vs ſee what we can do.   Exeunt.

Thunder.   Enter Lucifer and 4 deuils, *Fauſtus* to them
with this ſpeech.

    Fauſt. Now that the gloomy ſhadow of the night,
Longing to view Orions drizling looke,
Leapes from th'Antarticke world vnto the ſkie,
And dyms the Welkin, with her pitchy breathe:
Fauſtus, begin thine Incantations,
And try if deuils will obey thy Heſt,
Seeing thou haſt pray'd and ſacrific'd to them.
Within this circle is Iehoua's Name,
Forward, and backward, Anagramatiſ'd:
Th'abreuiated names of holy Saints,
Figures of euery adiunct to the heauens,
And Characters of Signes, and euening Starres,
By which the ſpirits are inforc'd to riſe :
Then feare not Fauſtus to be reſolute
And try the vtmoſt Magicke can performe.

Thunder, Siut mihi Dij Acherontis propitij, valeat numen tri-
plex Iehouæ, ignei Aerij, Aquatani ſpiritus ſaluete: Orientis
Princeps Belzebub, inferni ardentis monarcha & demigor-
gon, propitiamus vos, vt appareat, & ſurgat Mephoſtophilis
Dragon, quod tumeraris ; per Iehouam, gehennan, & con-
                         B   ſecratam

secratam aquam, quam nunc spargo; signumǿ; crucis quod
nunc facio; & per vota nostra ipse nunc surgat nobis dicatis
Mephostophilis.

260

Enter a Deuill.

I charge thee to returne, and change thy shape,
Thou art too vgly to attend on me:
Go and returne an old Franciscan Frier,
That holy shape becomes a deuill best.   Exit deuill.
I see there's vertue in my heauenly words.
Who would not be proficient in this Art?
How pliant is this Mephostophilis?
Full of obedience and humility,
Such is the force of Magicke, and my spels.

270

Enter Mephostophilis.

Meph. Now Faustus what wouldst thou haue me doe?
Faust. I charge thee waite vpon me whilst I liue
To do what euer Faustus shall command:
Be it to make the Moone drop from her Sphere,
Or the Ocean to ouerwhelme the world.
Meph. I am a seruant to great Lucifer,
And may not follow thee without his leaue;
No more then he commands, must we performe.
Faust. Did not he charge thee to appeare to me?
Meph. No, I came now hether of mine owne accord.
Faust. Did not my coniuring raise thee? speake.
Meph. That was the cause, but yet per accident:
For when we heare one racke the name of God,
Abiure the Scriptures, and his Sauiour Christ:
We flye in hope to get his glorious soule;
Nor will we come vnlesse he vse such meanes,
Whereby he is in danger to be damn'd:
Therefore the shortest cut for coniuring
Is stoutly to abiure all godlinesse,
And pray deuoutely to the Prince of hell.   (ple,
Faust. So Faustus hath already done, and holds this princi-
There is no chiefe but onely Beelzebub:

280

290

To

To whom Faustus doth dedicate himselfe.
This word Damnation, terrifies not me,
For I confound hell in Elizium :
My Ghost be with the old Phylosophers.
But leauing these vaine trifles of mens soules,
Tell me, what is that Lucifer, thy Lord?

Meph. Arch-regent and Commander of all Spirits.
Faust. Was not that Lucifer an Angell once?
Meph. Yes Faustus, and most deerely lou'd of God.
Faust. How comes it then that he is Prince of Deuils?
Meph. O : by aspiring pride and insolence,
For which God threw him from the face of heauen.
Faust. And what are you that liue with Lucifer?
Meph. Vnhappy spirits that liue with Lucifer,
Conspir'd against our God with Lucifer,
And are for euer damn'd with Lucifer.
Faust. Where are you damn'd? Meph. In hell.
Faust. How comes it then that thou art out of hell?
Meph. Why this is hell : nor am I out of it.
Think'st thou that I that saw the face of God,
And tasted the eternall Ioyes of heauen,
Am not tormented with ten thousand hels,
In being depriu'd of euerlasting blisse?
O Faustus leaue these friuolous demandes,
Which strikes a terror to my fainting soule.
Faust. What is great Mephostophilis so passionate
For being depriued of the Ioyes of heauen?
Learne thou of Faustus manly fortitude,
And scorne those Ioyes thou neuer shalt possesse.
Go beare these tydings to great Lucifer,
Seeing Faustus hath incur'd eternall death,
By desperate thoughts against Ioues Deity :
Say he surrenders vp to him his soule,
So he will spare him foure and twenty yeares,
Letting him liue in all voluptuousnesse,
Hauing thee euer to attend on me,
To giue me whatsoeuer I shall aske;
To tell me whatsoeuer I demand :

To slay mine enemies, and to aid my friends,
And alwaies be obedient to my will.
Go, and returne to mighty Lucifer,
And meet me in my Study, at Midnight,
And then resolue me of thy Maisters mind.

 Meph. I will Faustus.   Exit.

 Faust. Had I as many soules, as there be Starres,
I'de giue them all for Mephostophilis.
By him, I'le be great Emperour of the world,
And make a bridge, through the mouing Aire,
To passe the Ocean: with a band of men
I'le ioyne the Hils that bind the Affrick shore,
And make that Country, continent to Spaine,
And both contributary to my Crowne.
The Emperour shall not liue, but by my leaue,
Nor any Potentate of Germany.
Now that I haue obtain'd what I desir'd
I'le liue in speculation of this Art
Till Mephostophilis returne againe.   Exit.

Enter Wagner and the Clowne.

 Wag. Come hither sirra boy.
 Clo. Boy? O disgrace to my person: Zounds boy in your
face, you haue seene many boyes with beards I am sure.
 Wag. Sirra, hast thou no commings In?
 Clow. Yes, and goings out too, you may see sir.
 Wag. Alas poore slaue, see how pouerty iests in his naked-
nesse, I know the Villaines out of seruice, and so hungry,
that I know he would giue his soule to the deuill, for a shoul-
der of Mutton, tho it were bloud raw.
 Clo. Not so neither; I had need to haue it well rosted,
and good sauce to it, if I pay so deere, I can tell you.
 Wag. Sirra, wilt thou be my man and waite on me: and
I will make thee go, like Qui mihi discipulus.
 Clow. What, in Verse?
 Wag. No slaue, in beaten silke, and Staues-aker.
 Clow. Staues-aker? that's good to kill Vermine: then be-
like

12

like if I serue you, I shall be lousy.

Wag. Why so thou shalt be, whether thou dost it or no: for sirra, if thou dost not presently bind thy selfe to me for seuen yeares, I'le turne all the lice about thee into Familiars, and make them teare thee in peeces.

Clow. Nay sir, you may saue your selfe a labour, for they are as familiar with me, as if they payd for their meate and drinke, I can tell you.

Wag. Well sirra, leaue your iesting, and take these Guil-

Clow. Yes marry sir, and I thanke you to.   (ders.

Wag. So, now thou art to bee at an howres warning, whensoeuer, and wheresoeuer the deuill shall fetch thee.

Clow. Here, take your Guilders I'le none of 'em.

Wag. Not I, thou art Prest, prepare thy selfe, for I will presently raise vp two deuils to carry thee away: Banio, Belcher.

Clow. Belcher? and Belcher come here, I'le belch him: I am not afraid of a deuill.   Enter 2 deuils.

Wag. How now sir will you serue me now?

Clow. I good Wagner take away the deuill then.

Wag. Spirits away; now sirra follow me.

Clow. I will sir; but hearke you Maister, will you teach me this coniuring Occupation?

Wag. I sirra, I'le teach thee to turne thy selfe to a Dog, or a Cat, or a Mouse, or a Rat, or any thing.

Clow. A Dog, or a Cat, or a Mouse, or a Rat: O braue Wagner.

Wag. Villaine, call me Maister Wagner, and see that you walke attentiuely, and let your right eye be alwaies, Dia-m•trally fixt vpon my left heele, that thou maist, Quasi vesti-gias nostras insistere.

Clow. Well sir, I warrant you.   Exeunt.

Enter Faustus in his Study.

Faust. Now Faustus, must thou needs be damn'd?
Canst thou not be sau'd?
What bootes it then to thinke on God or Heauen?

Away with such vaine fancies, and despaire,
Despaire in G o d, and trust in Belzebub,
Now go not backward Faustus, be resolute.
Why wauerst thou? O something soundeth in mine eare.
Abiure this Magicke, turne to God againe.   (appetite
Why he loues thee not: The God thou seru'st is thine owne
Wherein is fixt the loue of Belzebub,
To him, I'le build an Altar and a Church,
And offer luke-warme bloud, of new borne babes.

Enter the two Angels.

Euill An. Go forward Faustus in that famous Art.
Good An. Sweete Faustus leaue that execrable Art.
Faust. Contrition, Prayer, Repentance? what of these?
Good A. O they are meanes to bring thee vnto heauen.
Bad A. Rather illusions, fruits of lunacy.
That make them foolish that do vse them most.
Good A. Sweet Faustus think of heauen, & heauenly things.
Bad A. No Faustus thinke of honour and of wealth. Ex.An.
Faust. Wealth? Why the Signory of Embden shall be mine:
When Mephostophilis shall stand by me,
What power can hurt me? Faustus thou art safe.
Cast no more doubts; Mepho: come
And bring glad tydings from great Lucifer.
Ist not midnight? come Mephostophilis.
Veni veni Mephostophile.   Enter Mephosto.
Now tell me what saith Lucifer thy Lord.
M. That I shall waite on Faustus whilst he liues,
So he will buy my seruice with his soule.
Faust. Already Faustus hath hazarded that for thee.
Meph. But now thou must bequeath it solemnly,
And wright a Deed of Gift with thine owne bloud;
For that security craues Lucifer.
If thou deny it I must backe to hell.
Faust. Stay Mephosto. and tell me,
What good will my soule do thy Lord?
Meph. Enlarge his kingdome.

410
420
430

14

Fauſt. Is that the reaſon why he tempts vs thus?

Meph. Solamen miseris, socios habuisse doloris.

Fauſt. Why, haue you any paine that torture other?

Meph. As great as haue the humane ſoules of men.
But tell me Fauſtus, ſhall I haue thy ſoule?
And I will be thy ſlaue and waite on thee,
And giue thee moze then thou haſt wit to aſke.

Fauſt. I Mephoſtophilis, I'le giue it him.

Meph. Then Fauſtus ſtab thy Arme couragiouſly,
And bind thy ſoule, that at ſome certaine day
Great Lucifer may claime it as his owne,
And then be thou as great as Lucifer.   (arme,

Fauſt. Loe Mephoſto: foz loue of thee Fauſtus hath cut his
And with his properblou d aſſures his ſoule to be great Luci-
Chiefe Lozd and Regent of perpetuall night.   (fers,
View here this bloud that trickles from mine arme,
And let it be propitious foz my wiſh.

Meph. But Fauſtus
Wzite it in manner of a Deed of Gift.

Fauſt. I ſo I do; but Mephoſtophilis
My bloud congeales, and I can wzite no moze.

Meph. I'le fetch thee fire to diſſolue it ſtreight.   Exit.

Fauſt. What might the ſtaying of my bloud poztend?
Is it vnwilling I ſhould wzite this byll?
Why ſtreames it not, that I may wzite a freſh?
Fauſtus giues to thee his ſoule: O there it ſtaid.
Why ſhouldſt thou not? is not thy ſoule thine owne?
Then wzite again: Fauſtus giues to thee his ſoule.

Enter Mephoſtoph: with the Chafer of Fire.

Meph. See Fauſtus here is fire, ſet it on.

Fauſt. So, now the bloud begins to cleere againe:
Now will I make an end immediately.

Meph. What will not I do to obtaine his ſoule?

Fauſt. Consummatum eſt : this byll is ended,
And Fauſtus hath bequeath'd his ſoule to Lucifer.
But what is this Inſcription on mine Arme?

15

Homo fuge, whether should I flye?
If vnto heauen, hee'le throw me downe to hell.
My sences are deceiu'd, here's nothing writ:
O yes, I see it plaine, euen heere is writ
Homo fuge, yet shall not Faustus flye.
 Meph. I'le fetch him somewhat to delight his minde.

Exit.

Enter Deuils, giuing Crownes and rich apparell to
Faustus : they dance, and then depart.
Enter Mephostophilis.

 Faust. What meanes this shew? speake Mephostophilis.
 Meph. Nothing Faustus but to delight thy mind,
And let thee see what Magicke can performe.
 Faust. But may I raise such spirits when I please?
 Meph. I Faustus, and do greater things then these.
 Faust. Then Mephostophilis receiue this scrole,
A Deed of Gift, of body and of soule:
But yet conditionally, that thou performe
All Couenants, and Articles, betweene vs both.
 Meph. Faustus, I sweare by Hell and Lucifer,
To effect all promises betweene vs both.
 Faust. Then heare me read it Mephostophilis.
On these conditions following.

First, that Faustus may be a spirit in forme and substance.
 Secondly, that Mephostophilis shall be his seruant, and be by him commanded.
 Thirdly, that Mephostophilis shall doe for him, and bring him whatsoeuer.
 Fourthly, that he shall be in his chamber or house inuisible.
 Lastly, that hee shall appeare to the said Iohn Faustus, at all times, in what shape and forme soeuer he please.
 I Iohn Faustus of Wittenberg, Doctor, by these presents, doe giue both body and soule to Lucifer, Prince of rhe East, and his Minister Mephastophilis, and furthermore grant vnto them that foure and twentie yeares being expired, and these Articles aboue written being inviolate, full power to fetch or carry the

said Iohn Faustus, body and soule, flesh, bloud, into their ha-
bitation wheresoeuer.

By me *Iohn Faustus.*

Meph. Speake Faustus, do you deliuer this as your Deed?

Faust. I take it, and the deuill giue thee good of it.

Meph. So, now Faustus aske me what thou wilt.

Faust. First, I will question thee about hell:
Tell me, where is the place that men call Hell?

Meph. Under the heauens.

Faust. I, so are all things else; but whereabouts?

Meph. Within the bowels of these Elements,
Where we are tortur'd, and remaine for euer.
Hell hath no limits, nor is circumscrib'd,
In one selfe place: but where we are is hell,
And where hell is there must we euer be.
And to be short, when all the world dissolues,
And euery creature shall be purifi'd,
All places shall be hell that is not heauen.

Faust. I thinke Hel's a fable.

Meph. I, thinke so still, till experience change thy mind.

Faust. Why, dost thou think that Faustus shall be damn'd?

Meph. I, of necessity, for here's the scrowle
In which thou hast giuen thy soule to Lucifer.

Faust. I, and body too, but what of that:
Think'st thou that Faustus, is so fond to imagine,
That after this life there is any paine?
No, these are trifles, and meere old wiues Tales.

Meph. But I am an instance to proue the contrary:
For I tell thee I am damn'd, and now in hell.

Faust. Nay, and this be hell, I'le willingly be damn'd.
What sleeping, eating, walking and disputing?
But leauing this, let me haue a wife, the fairest Maid in
Germany, for I am wanton and lasciuious, and cannot liue
without a wife.

Meph. Well Faustus, thou shalt haue a wife.

He fetches in a woman deuill.

Faust. What sight is this?

C   Meph.

17

Meph. Now Fauſtus wilt thou haue a wife?

Fauſt. Here's a hot whoze indœd; no, I'le no wife.

Meph. Marriage is but a ceremoniall toy,

And if thou loueſt me thinke no moze of it,

I'le cull thee out the faireſt Curtezans,

And bzing them euery mozning to thy bed:

She whom thine eye ſhall like, thy heart ſhall haue,

Were ſhe as chaſte as was Penelope,

As wiſe as Saba, oz as beautifull

As was bzight Lucifer befoze his fall.

Here, take this booke, and peruſe it well:

The Iterating of theſe lines bzings gold,

The framing of this circle on the ground

Bzings Thunder, Whirle-winds, Stozme and Lightning:

Pzonounce this thzice deuoutly to thy ſelfe,

And men in harneſſe ſhall appeare to thee,

Ready to erecute what thou commandſt.

Fauſt. Thankes Mephoſtophilis foz this ſweete booke,

This will I keepe, as chary as my life.   Exeunt.

Enter Wagner ſolus.

Wag. Learned Fauſtus

To know the ſecrets of Aſtronomy

Grauen in the booke of Ioues high firmament,

Did mount himſelfe to ſcale Olympus top,

Being ſeated in a chariot burning bzight,

Drawne by the ſtrength of yoaky Dzagons necks,

He now is gone to pzoue Coſmography,

And as I geſſe will firſt arriue at Rome,

To ſee the Pope and manner of his Court,

And take ſome part of holy Peters feaſt,

That to this day is highly ſolemnized.   Exit Wagner.

Enter Fauſtus in his Study, and Mephoſtophilis.

Fauſt. When I behold the heauens then I repent

And curſe thee wicked Mephoſtophilis,

Becauſe

18

Because thou hast depriu'd me of those Ioyes.

   Meph. 'Twas thine own seeking Faustus, thanke thy selfe.
But think'st thou heauen is such a glorious thing?
I tell thee Faustus it is not halfe so faire
As thou, or any man that breathe on earth.

   Faust. How prou'st thou that?

   Meph. 'Twas made for man; then he's more excellent.

   Faust. If Heauen was made for man, 'twas made for me:
I will renounce this Magicke and repent.

Enter the two Angels.

   Good A. Faustus repent, yet God will pitty thee.
   Bad A. Thou art a spirit, God cannot pity thee.
   Faust. Who buzzeth in mine eares I am a spirit?
Be I a deuill yet God may pitty me.
Yea, God will pitty me if I repent.
   Euill An. I, but Faustus neuer shall repent.

                      Exit Angels.

   Faust. My heart is hardned, I cannot repent:
Scarce can I name saluation, faith, or heauen.
Swords, poyson, halters, and inuenomb'd steele,
Are laid before me to dispatch my selfe:
And long e're this, I should haue done the deed,
Had not sweete pleasure conquer'd deepe despaire.
Haue not I made blind Homer sing to me
Of Alexanders loue, and Oenons death?
And hath not he that built the walles of Thebes,
With rauishing sound of his melodious Harpe,
Made musicke with my Mephostophilis?
Why should I die then, or basely despaire?
I am resolu'd, Faustus shall not repent.
Come Mephostophilis let vs dispute againe,
And reason of diuine Astrology.
Speake, are there many Spheares aboue the Moone?
Are all Celestiall bodies but one Globe,
Is it the substance of this centricke earth?

                            Meph.

Meph. As are the elements, such are the heauens,
Euen from the Moone vnto the Emperiall Orbe,
Mutually folded in each others Spheares,
And iontly moue vpon one Axle-træ,
Whose termine, is tearmed the worlds wide Pole.
Nor are the names of Saturne, Mars, or Iupiter,
Fain'd, but are euening Starres.

Fauſt. But haue they all one motion, both situ & tempore?

Meph. All moue from Eaſt to Weſt, in foure and
twenty houres, vpon the poles of the world, but differ in
their motions vpon the poles of the Zodiacke.

Fauſt. Theſe ſlender queſtions Wagner can decide:
Hath Mephoſtophilis no greater ſkill?
Who knowes not the double motion of the Planets?
That the firſt is finiſht in a naturall day?
The ſecond thus, Saturne in 30 yeares;
Iupiter in 12, Mars in 4, the Sun, Venus, and
Mercury in a yeare; the Moone in twenty eight daies.
Theſe are freſh mens queſtions: But tell me, hath euery
Spheare a Dominion, or Intelligentia.   Meph. I.

Fauſt. How many Heauens, or Spheares, are there?

Meph. Nine, the seuen Planets, the Firmament, and the
Emperiall heauen.

Fauſt. But is there not Cœlum igneum, & Chriſtalinum?

Meph. No Fauſtus they be but Fables.

Fauſt. Reſolue me then in this one queſtion:
Why are not Coniunctions, Oppoſitions, Aſpects, Eclipſes,
all at one time, but in ſome yeares we haue moze, in ſome leſſe?

Meph. Per inæqualem motum, reſpectu totius.

Fauſt. Well, I am anſwer'd: now tell me who made the

Meph. I will not   (world?

Fauſt. Sweet Mephoſtophilis tell me.

Meph. Moue me not Fauſtus.

Fauſt. Uillaine, haue not I bound thee to tell me any thing?

Meph. I, that is not againſt our Kingdome.
This is: Thou art damn'd, think thou of hell.

Fauſt. Thinke Fauſtus vpon God, that made the world.

Meph. Remember this, ——— Exit.

20

620

630

640

650

Fauſt. I, go accurſed ſpirit to vgly hell:
'Tis thou haſt damn'd diſtreſſed Fauſtus ſoule. Iſt not to late?

Enter the two Angels.

Bad. Too late.
Good. Neuer too late, if Fauſtus will repent.
Bad. If thou repent, deuils will teare thee in peeces.
Good. Repent and they ſhall neuer raiſe thy ſkin. Ex. A.
Fauſt. O Chriſt my Sauiour, my Sauiour,
Helpe to ſaue diſtreſſed Fauſtus ſoule.

Enter Lucifer, Belzebub, and Mephoſtophilis.

Lucif. Chriſt cannot ſaue thy ſoule, for he is iuſt,
There's none but I haue intereſt in the ſame.
Fauſt. O what art thou that look'ſt ſo terribly.
Lucif. I am Lucifer, and this is my companion Prince in
Fauſt. O Fauſtus they are come to fetch thy ſoule.   (hell.
Belz. We are come to tell thee thou doſt iniure vs.
Lucif. Thou calſt on Chriſt contrary to thy promiſe.
Belſ. Thou ſhould'ſt not thinke on God.
Lucif. Thinke on the deuill.
Belz. And his dam to.
Fauſt. Nor will Fauſtus henceforth: pardon him for this,
And Fauſtus vowes neuer to looke to heauen.
Lucif. So ſhalt thou ſhew thy ſelfe an obedient ſeruant,
And we will highly gratify thee for it.
Belz. Fauſtus we are come from hell in perſon to ſhew
thee ſome paſtime: ſit downe and thou ſhalt behold the ſeuen
deadly ſinnes appeare to thee in their owne proper ſhapes
and likeneſſe.
Fauſt. That ſight will be as pleaſant to me, as Paradiſe
was to Adam the firſt day of his creation.
Lucif. Talke not of Paradice or Creation, but marke
the ſhew, go Mephoſtoph. fetch them in.

Enter the 7 deadly ſinnes.

Belz. Now Fauſtus, queſtion them of their names and
diſpoſitions.
                                                    Fauſt.

Fauſt. That ſhall I ſoone: What art thou the firſt?

Pride. I am Pride; I diſdaine to haue any parents: I am like to Ouids Flea, I can creepe into euery corner of a Wench: Sometimes, like a Perriwig, I ſit vpon her Brow: next, like a Necke-lace I hang about her Necke: Then, like a Fan of Feathers, I kiſſe her; And then turning my ſelfe to a wrought Smocke do what I liſt. But fye, what a ſmell is heere? I'le not ſpeake a word more for a kings ranſoms, vnleſſe the ground be perfum'd, and couer'd with cloth of Arras.

Fauſt. Thou art a proud knaue indeed: What art thou the ſecond?

Couet. I am Couetouſneſſe: begotten of an old Churle in a leather bag; and might I now obtaine my wiſh, this houſe you and all, ſhould turne to Gold, that I might locke you ſafe into my Cheſt: O my ſweete Gold!

Fauſt. And what art thou the third?

Enuy. I am Enuy, begotten of a Chimney-ſweeper, and an Oyſter-wife: I cannot read, and therefore wiſh all books burn'd. I am leane with ſeeing others eate: O that there would come a famine oner all the world, that all might die, and I liue alone: then thou ſhould'ſt ſee how fat I de be. But muſt thou ſit, and I ſtand? come downe with a vengeance.

Fauſt. Out enuious wretch: But what art thou the fourth?

Wrath. I am Wrath, I had neither father nor mother, I leapt out of a Lyons mouth when I was ſcarce an houre old, and euer ſince haue run vp and downe the world with theſe caſe of Rapiers, wounding my ſelfe when I could get none to fight withall: I was borne in hell, and look to it, for ſome of you ſhall be my father.

Fauſt. And what art thou the fift?

Glut. I am Gluttony; my parents are all dead, and the deuill a peny they haue left me, but a ſmall pention, and that buyes me thirty meales a day, and ten Beauers: a ſmall trifle to ſuffice nature. I come of a Royall Pedigree, my father was a Gammon of Bacon, and my mother was a Hogs-head of Claret Wine. My godfathers were theſe: Peter-pickeld-herring, and Martin Martlemaſſe-beefe: But my god

700

710

720

22

mother, Ȣ ſhe was an ancient Gentlewoman, her name was
Margery March-beere: Now Fauſtus thou haſt heard all my
progeny, wilt thou bid me to ſuppet?

Fauſt. Not I.

Glu Then the deuill chooke thee.

Fauſt. Choke thy ſelfe Glutton: What art thou the ſirt?

Sloth. Hey ho: I am Sloth: I was begotten on a ſunny-
bank: hey ho: Ile not ſpeak a word more for a kings ranſome.

Fau. And what are you Miſtris Minkes, the ſeuenth & laſt?

Letch. Who I I ſir? I am one that loues an inch of raw
Mutton, better then an ell of fryde Stockfiſh: and the firſt
letter of my name begins with Letchery.

Luc. Away to hell, away on piper.   Ex. the 7 ſinnes.

Fauſt. O how this ſight doth delight my ſoule.

Luc. But Fauſtus, in hell is all manner of delight.

Fauſt. O might I ſee hell, and returne againe ſafe, how
happy were I then.

Luc. Fauſtus, thou ſhalt, at midnight I will ſend for thee;
Meane while peruſe this booke, and view it throughly,
And thou ſhalt turne thy ſelfe into what ſhape thou wilt.

Fauſt. Thankes mighty Lucifer:
This will I keepe as chary as my life.

Luc. Now Fauſtus farewell.

Fauſt. Farewell great Lucifer: come Mephoſtophilis
                                   Exeunt omnes, ſeuerall waies.

Enter the Clowne.

What Dick, looke to the horſes there till I come againe.
I haue gotten one of Doctor Fauſtus coniuring bookes, and
now we'le haue ſuch knauery, as't paſſes.

Enter Dick.

Dick. What Robin, you muſt come away & walk the horſes.

Rob. I walke the horſes, I ſcorn't 'faith, I haue other
matters in hand, let the horſes walk themſelues and they will.
A per ſe a, t. h. e the: o per ſe o deny orgon, gorgon: keepe
further from me O thou illiterate, and vnlearned Hoſtler.

Dick. Snayles, what haſt thou got there a book: why thou
canſt not tell ne're a word on't.

                                                        Rob.

Rob. That thou shalt see presently: keep out of the circle, I say, least I send you into the Ostry with a vengeance.

Dick. That's like 'faith: you had best leaue your foolery, for an my Maister come, he'le coniure you 'faith.

Rob. My Maister coniure me? I'le tell thee wh̄ an my Maister come here, I'le clap as faire a paire of ... es on'ꝭ head as e're thou sawest in thy life.

Dick. Thou needst not do that, for my Mistresse hath done ...

Rob. I, there be of vs here, that haue waded as deepe into matters, as other men, if they were disposed to talke.

Dick. A plague take you, I thought you did not sneake vp and downe after her for nothing. But I prethee tell me, in good sadnesse Robin, is that a coniuring booke?

Rob. Do but speake what thou't haue me to do, and I'le do't: If thou't dance naked, put off thy cloathes, and I'le coniure thee about presently: Or if thou't go but to the Tauerne with me, I'le giue thee white wine, red wine, claret wine, Sacke, Muskadine, Malmesey and Whippincrust, hold belly hold, and wee'le not pay one peny for it.

Dick. O braue, prethee let's to it presently, for I am as dry as a dog.

Rob. Come then let's away.   Exeunt.

Enter the Chorus.

Learned Faustus to find the secrets of Astronomy,
Grauen in the booke of Ioues high firmament,
Did mount him vp to scale Olimpus top.
Where sitting in a Chariot burning bright,
Drawne by the strength of yoked Dragons neckes;
He viewes the cloudes, the Planets, and the Starres,
The Tropick, Zones, and quarters of the skye,
From the bright circle of the horned Moone,
Euen to the height of Primum Mobile:
And whirling round with this circumference,
Within the concaue compasse of the Pole,
From East to West his Dragons swiftly glide,
And in eight daies did bring him home againe.

Not long he stayed within his quiet house,
To rest his bones after his weary toyle,
But new exploits do hale him out agen,
And mounted then vpon a Dragons backe,
That with his wings did part the subtle aire:
He now is gone to proue Cosmography,
That measures costs, and kingdomes of the earth:
And as I guesse will first arriue at Rome,
To see the Pope and manner of his Court,
And take some part of holy Peters feast,
The which this day is highly solemnized.　　　　Exit.

Enter Faustus and Mephostophilis.

Faust. Hauing now my good Mephostophilis,
Past with delight the stately Towne of Trier:
Inuironed round with airy mountaine tops,
With wals of Flint, and deepe intrenched Lakes,
Not to be wonne by any conquering Prince.
From Paris next, costing the Realme of France,
We saw the Riuer Maine, fall into Rhines,
Whose bankes are set with Groues of fruitfull Uines.
Then vp to Naples, rich Campania,
Whose buildings faire, and gorgeous to the eye,
The streetes straight forth, and paued with finest bricke.
There saw we learned Maroes golden tombe:
The way he cut an English mile in length,
Through a rocke of stone in one nights space:
From thence to Venice, Padua, and the East,
In one of which a sumptuous Temple stands,
That threates the starres with her aspiring top,
Whose frame is paued with sundry coloured stones,
And roof't aloft with curious worke in gold.
Thus hitherto hath Faustus spent his time.
But tell me now, what resting place is this?
Hast thou, as earst I did command,
Conducted me within the walles of Rome?
　　Meph. I haue my Faustus, and for proofe thereof,
　　　　　　　　　　D　　　　　　　　　　　This

25

This is the goodly Palace of the Pope :
And cause we are no common guests,
I chuse his priuy chamber for our vse.

    Faust. I hope his Holinesse will bid vs welcome.

    Meph. All's one, for wee'l be bold with his Venson.
But now my Faustus, that thou maist perceiue,
What Rome containes for to delight thine eyes.
Know that this City stands vpon seuen hils,
That vnderprop the ground-worke of the same:
Iust through the midst runnes flowing Tybers streame,
With winding bankes that cut it in two parts ;
Ouer the which two stately Bridges leane,
That make safe passage, to each part of Rome.
Vpon the Bridge, call'd Ponto Angelo,
Erected is a Castle passing strong,
Where thou shalt see such store of Ordinance,
As that the double Cannons forg'd of brasse,
Do watch the number of the daies contain'd,
Within the compasse of one compleat yeare :
Beside the gates, and high Pyramydes,
That Iulius Cæsar brought from Affrica.

    Faust. Now by the kingdomes of Infernall Rule,
Of Stix, of Acheron, and the fiery Lake,
Of euer-burning Phlegeton, I sweare,
That I do long to see the Monuments
And situation of bright splendent Rome,
Come therefore, let's away.

    Meph. Nay stay my Faustus : I know you'd see the Pope
And take some part of holy Peters feast,
The which this day with high solemnity,
This day is held through Rome and Italy ,
In honour of the Popes triumphant victory.

    Faust. Sweete Mephosto. thou pleasest me
Whilst I am here on earth : Let me be cloyd
With all things that delight the heart of man.
My foure and twenty yeares of liberty
I'le spend in pleasure and in daliance,
That Faustus name, whilst this bright frame doth stand,

May be admired through the furthest Land.

Meph. 'Tis well said Faustus, come then stand by me
And thou shalt see them come immediately.

Faust. Nay stay my gentle Mephostophilis,
And grant me my request, and then I go.
Thou know'st within the compasse of eight daies,
We veiw'd the face of heauen, of earth and hell.
So high our Dragons soar'd into the aire,
That looking downe the earth appear'd to me,
No bigger then my hand in quantity.
There did we view the kingdomes of the world,
And what might please mine eye, I there beheld.
Then in this shew let me an Actor be,
That this proud Pope may Faustus comming see.

Meph. Let it be so my Faustus, but first stay,
And view their triumphs, as they passe this way.
And then deuise what best contents thy minde,
By comming in thine Art to crosse the Pope,
Or dash the pride of this solemnity;
To make his Monkes and Abbots stand like Apes,
And point like Antiques at his triple Crowne :
To beate the beades about the Friers Pates,
Or clap huge hornes, vpon the Cardinals heads:
Or any villany thou canst deuise,
And I'le performe it Faustus : hearke they come :
This day shall make thee be admir'd in Rome.

Enter the Cardinals and Bishops, some bearing Crosiers, some
the Pillars, Monkes and Friers, singing their Procession:
Then the Pope, and Raymond King of Hunga-
ry, with Bruno led in chaines.

Pope. Cast downe our Foot-stoole.

Ray. Saxon Bruno stoope,
Whilst on thy backe his hollinesse ascends
Saint Peters Chaire and State Pontificall.

Bru. Proud Lucifer, that State belongs to me:
But thus I fall to Peter, not to thee.

D 2

Pope

27

Pope Come and Peter, shalt thou groueling lie,
And crouch before the Papall dignity :
Sound Trumpets then, for thus Saint Peters Heire,
From Bruno's backe, ascends Saint Peters Chaire.
        A Flourish while he ascends.
Thus, as the Gods, creepe on with feete of wooll,
Long ere with Iron hands they punish men,
So shall our sleeping vengeance now arise,
And smite with death thy hated enterprise.
Lord Cardinals of France and Padua,
Go forth-with to our holy Consistory,
And read amongst the Statutes Decretall,
What by the holy Councell held at Trent,
The sacred Sinod hath decreed for him,
That doth assume the Papall gouernment,
Without election, and a true consent :
Away and bring vs word with speed.
    1 Card. We go my Lord.   Exeunt Cardinals.
    Pope. Lord Raymond.
    Faust. Go haste thee gentle Mephostophilis,
Follow the Cardinals to the Consistory ;
And as they turne their superstitious Bookes ,
Strike them with sloth, and drowsy idlenesse;
And make them sleepe so sound, that in their shapes,
Thy selfe and I, may parly with this Pope :
This proud confronter of the Emperour,
And in despits of all his Holinesse
Restore this Bruno to his liberty,
And beare him to the States of Germany.
    Meph. Faustus, I goe.
    Faust. Dispath it soone,
The Pope shall curse that Faustus came to Rome.
                            Exit Faustus and Meph.
    Bruno. Pope Adrian let me haue some right of Law,
I was elected by the Emperour.
    Pope. We will depose the Emperour for that deed,
And curse the people that submit to him ;
Both he and thou shalt stand excommunicate,

28

And interdict from Churches priuiledge,
And all society of holy men:
He growes to proud in his authority,
Lifting his loftie head aboue the clouds,
And like a Steeple ouer-peeres the Church.
But wee'le pul downe his haughty insolence:
And as Pope Alexander our Progenitour,
Trode on the neck of Germane Fredericke,
Adding this golden sentence to our praise;
That Peters heires should tread on Emperours,
And walke vpon the dreadfull Adders backe,
Treading the Lyon, and the Dragon downe.
And fearelesse spurne the killing Basiliske:
So will we quell that haughty Schismatique;
And by authority Apostolicall
Depose him from his Regall Gouernment.
　Bru.　Pope Iulius swore to Princely Sigismond,
For him, and the succeeding Popes of Rome,
To hold the Emperours their lawfull Lords.
　Pope.　Pope Iulius did abuse the Churches Rites,
And therefore none of his Decrees can stand.
Is not all power on earth bestowed on vs?
And therefore tho we would we cannot erre.
Behold this Siluer Belt whereto is firt
Seuen golden seales fast sealed with seuen seales,
In token of our seuen-fold power from heauen,
To binde or loose, lock fast, condemne, or iudge,
Resigne, or seale, or what so pleaseth vs.
Then he and thou, and all the world shall stoope,
Or be assured of our dreadfull curse,
To light as heauy as the paines of hell.

　　Enter Faustus and Mephosto. like the Cardinals.

　Meph.　Now tell me Faustus, are we not fitted well?
　Faust.　Yes Mephosto. and two such Cardinals
Ne're seru'd a holy Pope, as we shall do.
But whilst they sleepe within the Consistory,
　　　　　D 3　　　　　　　　　　　　　Let

29

Let vs salute his reuerend Father-hœd.

Ray. Behold my Lord, the Cardinals are return'd.

Pope. Welcome graue Fathers, answere presently,
What haue our holy Councell there decreed,
Concerning Bruno and the Emperour,
In quittance of their late conspiracie
Against our State, and Papall dignitie?

Faust. Most sacred Patron of the Church of Rome,
By full consent of all the Synod
Of Priests and Prelates, it is thus decreed:
That Bruno, and the Germane Emperour
Be held as Lollords, and bold Schismatiques,
And proud disturbers of the Churches peace.
And if that Bruno by his owne assent,
Without inforcement of the German Peeres,
Did seeke to weare the triple Dyadem,
And by your death to clime S. Peters Chaire.,
The Statutes Decretall haue thus decreed,
He shall be streight condemn'd of heresie,
And on a pile of Fagots burnt to death.

Pope. It is enough: here, take him to your charge,
And beare him streight to Ponto Angelo,
And in the strongest Tower inclose him fast,
To morrow, sitting in our Consistory,
With all our Colledge of graue Cardinals,
We will determine of his life or death.
Here, take his triple Crowne along with you,
And leaue it in the Churches treasury.
Make haste againe, my good Lord Cardinalls,
And take our blessing Apostolicall.

Meph. So, so, was neuer Diuell thus blest before.

Faust. Away sweet Mephosto, be gone,
The Cardinals will be plagu'd for this anon. Ex. Fa. & Mep.

Pope. Go presently, and bring a banket forth,
That we may solemnize S. Peters feast,
And with Lord Raymond, King of Hungary,
Drinke to our late and happy victory. Exeunt.

A Senit while the Banquet is brought in; and then Enter
Fauſtus and Mephaſtophilis in their owne
ſhapes.

Meph. Now Fauſtus, come prepare thy ſelfe for mirth,
The ſleepy Cardinals are hard at hand,
To cenſure Bruno, that is poſted hence,
And on a proud pac'd Steed, as ſwift as thought,
Flies ore the Alpes to fruitfull Germany,
There to ſalute the wofull Emperour.
Fauſt. The Pope will curſe them for their ſloth to day,
That ſlept both Bruno and his crowne away,
But now, that Fauſtus may delight his minde,
And by their folly make ſome merriment,
Sweet Mephaſto: ſo charme me here,
That I may walke inuiſible to all,
And doe what ere I pleaſe, vnſeene of any.
Meph. Fauſtus thou ſhalt, then kneele downe preſently,
Whilſt on thy head I lay my hand,
And charme thee with this Magicke wand,
Firſt weare this girdle, then appeare
Inuiſible to all are here :
The Planets ſeuen, the gloomy aire,
Hell and the Furies forked haire,
Pluto's blew fire, and Hecat's tree,
With Magicke ſpels ſo compaſſe thee,
That no eye may thy body ſee.

So Fauſtus, now for all their holineſſe,
Do what thou wilt, thou ſhalt not be diſcern'd.
Fauſt. Thankes Mephaſto : now Friers take heed,
Leſt Fauſtus make your ſhauen crownes to bleed.
Meph. Fauſtus no more : ſee where the Cardinals come.

Enter Pope and all the Lords.   Enter the Cardinals
with a Booke.
Pope. Welcome Lord Cardinals : come ſit downe.

31

Lo2d Raymond, take your feate, Friers attend,
And see that all things be in readinesse,
As best beseemes this solemne festiuall.

   1.Card. First, may it please your sacred Holinesse,
To view the sentence of the reuerend Synod,
Concerning Bruno and the Emperour.

   Pope. What needs this question? Did I not tell you,
To mo2row we would sit i'th Consisto2y,
And there determine of his punishment?
You b2ought vs wo2d euen now, it was decreed,
That Bruno and the cursed Emperour
Were by the holy Councell both condemn'd
Fo2 lothed Lollo2ds, and base Schismatiques:
Then wherefo2e would you haue me view that booke?

   1.Card. Your Grace mistakes, you gaue vs no such charge.
   Ray. Deny it not, we all are witnesses
That 'Bruno here was late deliuered you,
With his rich triple crowne to be reseru'd,
And put into the Churches treasury.

   Amb.Card. By holy Paul we saw them not.
   Pope. By Peter you shall dye,
Unlesse you b2ing them fo2th immediatly:
Hale them to p2ison, lade their limbes with gyues;
False P2elates, fo2 this hatefull treachery,
Curst be your soules to hellish misery.

   Faust. So, they are safe: now Faustus to the feast,
The Pope had neuer such a frolicke guest.

   Pope. Lo2d Archbishop of Reames, sit downe with vs.
   Bish. I thanke your Holinesse.
   Faust. Fall to, the Diuell choke you an you spare.
   Pope. Who's that spoke? Friers looke about,
Lo2d Raymond p2ay fall too, I am beholding
To the Bishop of Millaine, fo2 this so rare a p2esent.
   Faust. I thanke you sir.
   Pope. How now? who snatch't the meat from me!
Uillaines why speake you not?
My good Lo2d Archbishop, heres a most daintie dish,
Was sent me from a Cardinall in France.

Fauſt. I'le haue that too.

Pope. What Lollards do attend our Hollineſſe,
That we receiue ſuch great indignity? fetch me ſome wine.

Fauſt. I, pray do, for Fauſtus is a dry.

Pope. Lord Kaymond, I drink vnto your grace.

Fauſt. I pledge your grace.

Pope. My wine gone to? yes Lubbers look about
And find the man that doth this villany,
Or by our ſanctitude you all ſhall die.
I pray my Lords haue patience at this
Troubleſome banquet.

Biſh. Pleaſe it your holineſſe, I thinke it be ſome Ghoſt
crept out of Purgatory, and now is come vnto your holineſſe for his pardon.

Pope. It may be ſo:
Go then command our Prieſts to ſing a Dirge,
To lay the fury of this ſame troubleſome ghoſt.

Fauſt. How now? muſt euery bit be ſpiced with a Croſſe?
Nay then take that.

Pope. O I am ſlaine, help me my Lords:
O come and help to beare my body hence:
Damb'd be this ſoule for euer, for this deed.
Exeunt the Pope and his traine.

Me. Now Fauſtus, what will you do now? for I can tell you
You'le be curſt with Bell, Booke, and Candle.

Fauſt. Bell, Booke, and Candle; Candle, Booke, and Bell,
Forward and backward, to curſe Fauſtus to hell.

Enter the Friers with Bell, Booke, and Candle,
for the Dirge.

1 Frier. Come brethren, let's about our buſineſſe with
good deuotion.
Curſed be he that ſtole his holineſſe meate from the Table.
Maledicat Dominus.
Curſed be he that ſtroke his holineſſe a blow the face.
Maledicat Dominus.
E   Curſed

33

Cursed be he that strucke fryer Sandelo a blow on the pate.

Maledicat Dom.

Cursed be he that disturbeth our holy Dirge.

Maledicat Dom.

Cursed be he that tooke away his holinesse wine.

Maledicat Dom.

Beate the Friers, fling fire worke among them,
and Exeunt.   Exeunt.

Enter Clowne and Dicke, with a Cup.

Dick. Sirra Robin, we were best looke that your deuill
can answere the stealing of this same cup, for the Vintners
boy followes vs at the hard heeles.

Rob. 'Tis no matter, let him come; an he follow vs, I'le so
coniure him, as he was neuer coniur'd in his life, I warrant
him: let me see the cup.

Enter Vintner.

Dick. Here 'tis: yonder he comes: Now Robin, now or
neuer shew thy cunning.

Vint. O, are you here? I am glad I haue found you, you
are a couple of fine companions: pray where's the cup you
stole from the Tauerne?

Rob. How, how? we steale a cup? take heed what you say,
we looke not like cup-stealers I can tell you.

Vint. Neuer deny't, for I know you haue it, and I'le
search you.

Rob. Search me? I and spare not: hold the cup Dick,
come, come, search me, search me.

Vint. Come on sirra, let me search you now.

Dick. I, I, do, do, hold the cup Robin, I feare not your
searching; we scorne to steale your cups I can tell you.

Vint. Neuer out face me for the matter, for sure the cup is
betweene you two.

Rob. Nay there you lie, 'tis beyond vs both.

Ving.

1130

1140

1150

1160

Vint. A plague take you, I thought 'twas your knauery to take it away : Come, giue it me againe.

Rob. I much, when can you tell: Dick, make me a circle, and ſtand cloſe at my backe, and ſtir not for thy life, Vintner you ſhall haue your cup anon, ſay nothing Dick: O per ſe o, demogorgon, Belcher and Mephoſtophilis.

Enter Mephoſtophilis.

Meph. You Princely Legions of infernall Rule, How am I vexed by theſe villaines Charmes? From Conſtantinople haue they brought me now, Onely for pleaſure of theſe damned ſlaues.

Rob. By Lady ſir, you haue had a ſhrowd iourney of it, will it pleaſe you to take a ſhoulder of Mutton to ſupper,and a Teſter in your purſe, and go backe againe.

Dick. I, I pray you heartily ſir; for wee cal'd you but in ieaſt I promiſe you.

Meph. To purge the raſhneſſe of this curſed deed, Firſt, be thou turned to this vgly ſhape, For Apiſh deeds transformed to an Ape.

Rob. O braue, an Ape? I pray ſir, let me haue the carrying of him about to ſhew ſome trickes.

Meph. And ſo thou ſhalt: be thou transform'd to a dog,and carry him vpon thy backe; away be gone.

Rob. A dog? that's excellent : let the Maids looke well to their porridge-pots, for I'le into the Kitchin preſently: come Dick, come.   Exeunt the two Clownes.

Meph. Now with the flames of euer-burning fire, I'le wing my ſelfe and forth-with flie amaine Vnto my Fauſtus to the great Turkes Court.   Exit.

Enter Martino, and Frederick at ſeuerall dores.

Mart. What ho, Officers, Gentlemen, Hye to the preſence to attend the Emperour, Good Fredericke ſee the roomes be voyded ſtraight,

C 2   His

His Maiesty is comming to the Hall;
Go backe, and see the State in readinesse.

Fre. But where is Bruno our elected Pope,
That on a furies back came post from Rome,
Will not his grace consort the Emperour.

Mart. O yes, and with him comes the Germane Coniurer,
The learned Faustus, fame of Wittenberge,
The wonder of the world for Magick Art;
And he intends to shew great Carolus,
The race of all his stout progenitors;
And bring in presence of his Maiesty,
The royall shapes and warlike semblances
Of Alexander and his beauteous Paramour.

Fre. Where is Benuolio?

Mart. Fast asleepe I warrant you,
He took his rouse with stopes of Rhennish wine,
So kindly yesternight to Bruno's health,
That all this day the sluggard keepes his bed.

Fre. See, see his window's ope, we'l call to him.

Mart. What hoe, Benuolio.

Enter Benuolio aboue at a window, in his
nightcap: buttoning.

Benu. What a deuill ayle you two?

Mar. Speak softly sir, least the deuil heare you:
For Faustus at the Court is late arriu'd,
And at his heeles a thousand furies waite,
To accomplish what soeuer the Doctor please.

Benu. What of this?

Mar. Come leaue thy chamber first, and thou shalt see
This Coniurer performe such rare exploits,
Before the Pope and royall Emperour,
As neuer yet was seene in Germany.

Benu. Has not the Pope enough of coniuring yet?
He was vpon the deuils backe late enough;
And if he be so farre in loue with him,

I would he would post with him to Rome againe.

Fred. Speake, wilt thou come and see this sport?

Ben. Not I.

Mar. Wilt thou stand in thy Window, and see it then?

Ben. I, and I fall not asleepe i'th meane time.

Mar. The Emperour is at hand, who comes to see
What wonders by blacke spels may compast be.

Ben. Well, go you attend the Emperour : I am content
for this once to thrust my head out at a window: for they say,
if a man be drunke ouer night, the Diuell cannot hurt him in
the morning: if that bee true, I haue a charme in my head,
shall controule him as well as the Coniurer, I warrant you.
                                                                    Exit.

A Senit. Charles the Germane Emperour, Bruno,
          Saxony, Faustus, Mephostophilis, Frede-
                ricke Martino, and Atten-
                        dants.

Emp. Wonder of men, renown'd Magitian,
Thrice learned Faustus, welcome to our Court.
This deed of thine, in setting Bruno free
From his and our professed enemy,
Shall adde more excellence vnto thine Art,
Then if by powerfull Necromantick spels,
Thou couldst command the worlds obedience :
For euer be belou'd of Carolus.
And if this Bruno thou hast late redeem'd,
In peace possesse the triple Diadem,
And sit in Peters Chaire, despite of chance,
Thou shalt be famous through all Italy,
And honour'd of the Germane Emperour.

Faust. These gracious words, most royall Carolus,
Shall make poore Faustus to his vtmost power,
Both loue and serue the Germane Emperour,
And lay his life at holy Bruno's feet.
For proofe whereof, if so your Grace be pleas'd,

                        E 3   Tho

The Doctor stands prepar'd, by power of Art,
To cast his Magicke charmes, that shall pierce through
The Ebon gates of euer-burning hell,
And hale the stubborne Furies from their caues,
To compasse whatsoere your grace commands.

Ben. Bloud he speakes terribly: but for all that, I doe not
greatly beléeue him, he lokes as like Coniurer as the Pope to
a Coster-monger.

Emp. Then Faustus as thou late didst promise vs,
We would behold that famous Conquerour,
Great Alexander, and his Paramour,
In their true shapes, and state Maiesticall,
That we may wonder at their excellence.

Faust. Your Maiesty shall see them presently,
Mephosto away.
And with a solemne noyse of trumpets sound,
Present before this royall Emperour,
Great Alexander and his beauteous Paramour.

Meph. Faustus I will.

Ben. Well M. Doctor, an your Diuels come not away
quickly, you shall haue me asléepe presently: zounds I could
eate my selfe for anger, to thinke I haue beene such an Asse
all this while, to stand gaping after the diuels Gouernor, and
can sée nothing.

Faust. Il'e make you feele something anon, if my Art faile
me not.
My Lord, I must forewarne your Maiesty,
That when my Spirits present the royall shapes
Of Alexander and his Paramour,
Your grace demand no questions of the King,
But in dumbe silence let them come and goe.

Emp. Be it as Faustus please, we are content.

Ben. I, I, and I am content too: and thou bring Alexander and his Paramour before the Emperour, Il'e be Acte-
on, and turne my selfe to a Stagge.

Faust. And Il'e play Diana, and send you the hornes presently.

1270

1280

1290

1300

A

Senit. Enter at one the Emperour Alexander, at the other
Darius; they meete, Darius is throwne downe, Alexander kils him; takes off his Crowne, and offering to goe
out, his Paramour meetes him, he embraceth her, and
ſets Darius Crowne vpon her head; and comming backe, both ſalute the Emperour,
who leauing his State, offers to em-
brace them, which Fauſtus ſeeing,
ſuddenly ſtaies him. Then trumpets ceaſe, and Muſicke
ſounds.

My gracious Lord, you doe forget your ſelfe,
Theſe are but ſhadowes, not ſubſtantiall.
    Emp. O pardon me, my thoughts are ſo rauiſhed
With ſight of this renowned Emperour,
That in mine armes I would haue compaſt him.
But Fauſtus, ſince I may not ſpeake to them,
To ſatisfie my longing thoughts at full,
Let me this tell thee: I haue heard it ſaid,
That this faire Lady, whileſt ſhe liu'd on earth,
Had on her necke a little wart, or mole;
How may I proue that ſaying to be true?
    Fauſt. Your Maieſty may boldly goe and ſee.
    Emp. Fauſtus I ſee it plaine,
And in this ſight thou better pleaſeſt me,
Then if I gain'd another Monarchie.
    Fauſt. Away, be gone.   Exit Show.
Sée, ſée, my gracious Lord, what ſtrange beaſt is yon, that
hruſts his head out at window.
    Emp. O wondrous ſight: ſée Duke of Saxony,
Two ſpreading hornes moſt ſtrangely faſtened
Vpon the head of yong Benvolio.
    Sax. What is he aſléepe, or dead?
    Fauſt. He ſléeps my Lord, but dreames not of his hornes.
    Emp. This ſport is excellent: wée'l call and wake him.
What ho, Benvolio.

                                      Ben.

Ben. A plague vpon you, let me sleepe a while.

Emp. I blame thee not to sleepe much, hauing such a head of thine owne.

Sax. Looke vp Benvolio, tis the Emperour calls.

Ben. The Emperour? where? O zounds my head.

Emp. Nay, and thy hornes hold, tis no mater for thy head, for that's arm'd sufficiently.

Fauſt. Why how now sir knight, what hang'd by the hornes? this most horrible: fie, fie, pull in your head for shame, let not all the world wonder at you.

Ben. Zounds Doctor, is this your villany?

Fauſt. O say not so sir: the Doctor has no skill,
No Art, no cunning, to present these Lords,
Or bring before this royall Emperour
The mightie Monarch, warlicke Alexander.
If Fauſtus do it, you are streight resolu'd,
In bold Acteons shape to turne a Stagge.
And therefore my Lord, so please your Maiesty,
Ile raise a kennelll of Hounds shall hunt him so,
As all his footmanship shall scarce preuaile,
To keepe his Carkasse from their bloudy phangs.
Ho, Belimote, Argiron, Asterote.

Ben. Hold, hold : zounds he'l raise vp a kennell of Diuels I thinke anon : good my Lord intreate for me : 'sbloud I am neuer able to endure these torments.

Emp. Then good M. Doctor,
Let me intreate you to remoue his hornes,
He has done penance now sufficiently.

Fauſt. My gracious Lord, not so much for iniury done to me, as to delight your Maiesty with some mirth: hath Fauſtus iuſtly requited this iniurious knight, which being all I desire, I am content to remoue his hornes. Mephaſtophilis, transforme him ; and hereafter sir, looke you speake well of Schollers.

Ben. Speake well of yee? 'sbloud and Schollers be such Cuckold-makers to clap hornes of honest mens heades o'this order, Ile nere truſt smooth faces, and small ruffes more. But

an I be not reueng'd for this, would I might be turn'd to a
gaping Oyster, and drinke nothing but salt water.

Emp. Come Faustus while the Emperour liues,
In recompence of this thy high desert,
Thou shalt command the state of Germany,
And liue belou'd of mightie Carolus.　Exeunt omnes.

Enter Benvolio, Martino, Fredericke, and
Souldiers.

Mar. Nay sweet Benvolio, let vs sway thy thoughts
From this attempt against the Coniurer.

Ben. Away, you loue me not, to vrge me thus,
Shall I let slip so great an iniury,
When euery seruile groome ieasts at my wrongs,
And in their rusticke gambals proudly say,
Benvolio's head was grac't with hornes to day?
O may these eye-lids neuer close againe,
Till with my sword I haue that Coniurer slaine.
If you will aid me in this enterprise,
Then draw your weapons, and be resolute:
If not, depart: here will Benvolio die,
But Faustus death shall quit my infamie.

Fred. Nay, we will stay with thee, betide what may,
And kill that Doctor if he come this way.

Ben. Then gentle Fredericke hie thee to the groue,
And place our seruants, and our followers
close in an ambush there behinde the trees,
By this (I know) the Coniurer is neere,
I saw him kneele, and kisse the Emperours hand,
And take his leaue, laden with rich rewards.
Then Souldiers boldly fight; if Faustus die,
Take you the wealth, leaue vs the victorie.

Fred. Come souldiers, follow me vnto the groue,
Who kils him shall haue gold, and endlesse loue.
Exit Frederick with the Souldiers.

Ben. My head is lighter then it was by th'hornes,
F　　　　　　　　　　　　　　But

41

But yet my heart moze ponderous then my head,
And pants vntill I sée that Coniurer dead.

Mar. Where shall we place our selues Benvolio?

Ben. Here will we stay to bide the first assault,
O were that damned Hell-hound but in place,
Thou soone shouldst sée me quit my foule disgrace.

Enter Fredericke.

Fred. Close, close, the Coniurer is at hand,
And all alone, comes walking in his gowne;
Be ready then, and strike the Peasant downe.

Ben. Mine be that honour then: now sword strike home,
For hornes he gaue, Il'e haue his head anone.

Enter Faustus with the false head.

Mar. Sée, sée, he comes.

Ben. No words: this blow ends all,
Hell take his soule, his body thus must fall.

Faust. Oh.

Fred. Grone you Master Doctor?

Ben. Breake may his heart with grones: déere Frederik sée
Thus will I end his griefes immediatly.

Mar. Strike with a willing hand, his head is off.

Ben. The Diuel's dead, the Furies now may laugh.

Fred. Was this that sterne aspect, that awfull frowne,
Made the grim monarch of infernall spirits,
Tremble and quake at his commanding charmes?

Mar. Was this that damned head, whose heart conspir'd
Benvolio's shame before the Emperour.

Ben. I, that's the head, and here the body lies,
Iustly rewarded for his villanies.

Fred. Come, let's deuise how we may adde moze shame
To the blacke scandall of his hated name.

Ben. First, on his head, in quittance of my wrongs,
Il'e naile huge forked hornes, and let them hang
Within the window where he yoak'd me first,
That all the world may sée my iust reuenge.

Mar. What vse shall we put his beard to?

Ben.

Ben. Wee'l sell it to a Chimny-sweeper: it will weare out ten birchin broomes I warrant you.

Fred. What shall eyes doe?

Ben. Wee'l put out his eyes, and they shall serue for buttons to his lips, to keepe his tongue from catching cold.

Mar. An excellent policie: and now sirs, hauing diuided him, what shall the body doe?

Ben. Zounds the Diuel's aliue agen.

Fred. Giue him his head for Gods sake.

Faust. Nay keepe it: Faustus will haue heads and hands,
I call your hearts to recompence this deed.
Knew you not Traytors, I was limitted
For foure and twenty yeares, to breathe on earth?
And had you cut my body with your swords,
Or hew'd this flesh and bones as small as sand,
Yet in a minute had my spirit return'd,
And I had breath'd a man made free from harme.
But wherefore doe I dally my reuenge?
Asteroth, Belimoth, Mephostophilis,   ⎱Ent. Meph. &
Go horse these traytors on your fiery backes,⎰other Diuels.
And mount aloft with them as high as heauen,
Thence pitch them headlong to the lowest heil:
Yet stay, the world shall see their miserie,
And hell shall after plague their treacherie.
Go Belimothe, and take this caitife hence,
And hurle him in some lake of mud and durt:
Take thou this other, dragge him through the woods,
Amongst the pricking thornes, and sharpest briers,
Whilst with my gentle Mephostophilis,
This Traytor flies vnto some steepie rocke,
That rowling downe, may breake the villaines bones,
As he intended to dismember me.
Fly hence, dispatch my charge immediatly.

Fred. Pitie vs gentle Faustus, saue our liues,

Faust. Away.

Fred. He must needs goe that the Diuell driues.

Exeunt Spirits with the knights.

F 2   Enter

Enter the ambusht Souldiers.

1 Sold. Come sirs, prepare your selues in readinesse,
Make hast to help these noble Gentlemen,
I heard them parly with the Coniurer.
2 Sold. See where he comes, dispatch, and kill the slaue.
Faust. What's here? an ambush to betray my life:
Then Faustus try thy skill: base pesants stand,
For loe these Trees remoue at my command,
And stand as Bulwarkes twixt your selues and me,
To sheild me from your hated treachery:
Yet to encounter this your weake attempt,
Behold an Army comes incontinent.

Faustus strikes the dore, and enter a deuill playing on a Drum,
    after him another bearing an Ensigne: and diuers with
    weapons, Mephostophilis with fire-workes; they set vpon
    the Souldiers and driue them out.

Enter at seuerall dores, Benuolio, Fredericke, and Martino,
    their heads and faces bloudy, and besmear'd with
    mud and durt; all hauing hornes on
                their heads.

Mart. What ho, Benuolio.
Benu. Here, what Frederick, ho.
Fred. O help me gentle friend; where is Martino?
Mart. Deere Frederick here,
Halfe smother'd in a Lake of mud and durt,
Through which the Furies drag'd me by the heeles.
Fred. Martino see,
Benuolio's hornes againe.
Mart. O misery, how now Benuolio?
Benu. Defend me heauen, shall I be haunted still?
Mart. Nay feare not man we haue no power to kill.
Benu. My friends transformed thus: O hellish spite,
                                                Your

44

Your heads are all ſet with hornes.

Fred. You hit it right,

It is your owne you meane feele on your head.

Benu. 'Zons, hornes againe.

Mart. Nay chafe not man, we all are ſped.

Benu. What deuill attends this damn'd Magician,

That ſpite of ſpite, our wrongs are doubled?

Fred. What may we do, that we may hide our ſhames?

Benu. If we ſhould follow him to worke reuenge,

He'dioyne long Aſſes eares to theſe huge hornes,

And make vs laughing ſtockes to all the world.

Mart. What ſhall we then do deere Benuolio?

Benu. I haue a Caſtle ioyning neere theſe woods,

And thither wee'le repaire and liue obſcure,

Till time ſhall alter this our brutiſh ſhapes:

With blacke diſgrace hath thus ecliptt our fame.

We'le rather die with griefe, then liue with ſhame.

Exeunt omnes.

Enter Fauſtus, and the Horſe-courſer, and
Mephoſtophilis.

Horſe. I beſeech your worſhip accept of theſe forty
Dollors.

Fauſt. Friend, thou canſt not buy ſo good a horſe, for ſo
mall a price: I haue no great need to ſell him, but if thou
keſt him for ten Dollors more, take him, becauſe I ſee thou
aſt a good minde to him.

Horſe. I beſeech you ſir accept of this; I am a very poore
man, and haue loſt very much of late by horſe fleſh, and this
argaine will ſet me vp againe.

Fauſt. Well, I will not ſtand with thee, giue me the mo-
ey: now ſirra I muſt tell you, that you may ride him o're
edge and ditch, and ſpare him not; but do you heare? in any
ſe, ride him not into the water.

Horſe. How ſir, not into the water? why will he not drink
all waters?

F 3

Fauſt.

45

The Tragicall Historie

Fauſt. Yes, he will dꝛinke of all waters, but ride him not into the water; oꝛ oꝛe hedge and ditch, oꝛ where thou wilt, but not into the water: Go bid the Hoſtler deliuer him vnto you, and remember what I ſay.

Horſe. I warrant you ſir; O ioyfull day : Now am I a made man foꝛ euer. _Exit._

Fauſt. What art thou Fauſtus but a man condemn'd to die? Thy fatall time dꝛawes to a finall end; Deſpaire doth dꝛiue diſtruſt into my thoughts. Confound theſe paſſions with a quiet ſleepe : Tuſh Chꝛiſt did call the Theefe vpon the Croſſe, Then reſt thee Fauſtus quiet in conceit.

He ſits to ſleepe.

Enter the Horſe-courſer wet.

Horſe. O what a coſening Doctoꝛ was this? I riding my hoꝛſe into the water, thinking ſome hidden myſtery had béene in the hoꝛſe, I had nothing vnder me but a little ſtraw, and had much ado to eſcape dꝛowning : Well I'le go rouſe him, and make him giue me my foꝛty Dolloꝛs againe. Ho ſirra Doctoꝛ, you coſoning ſcab; Maiſter Doctoꝛ awake, and riſe, and giue me my mony againe, foꝛ your hoꝛſe is turned to a bottle of Hay, —— Maiſter Doctoꝛ. He puls off his leg. Alas I am vndone, what ſhall I do? I haue puld off his leg.

Fauſt. O help, help, the villaine hath murder'd me.

Horſe. Murder oꝛ not murder , now he has but one leg, I'le out-run him, and caſt this leg into ſome ditch oꝛ other.

Fauſt. Stop him, ſtop him, ſtop him —— ha,ha,ha, Fauſtus hath his leg againe, and the Hoꝛſe-courſer a bundle of hay foꝛ his foꝛty Dolloꝛs.

Enter Wagner.

How now Wagner what newes with thee?

Wag. If it pleaſe you, the Duke of Vanholt doth earneſt-ly entreate your company, and hath ſent ſome of his men t' attend you with pꝛouiſion fit foꝛ your iourney.

Fauſt

1560

1570

1580

46

Faust. The Duke of Vanholt's an honourable Gentle-
man, and one to whom I must be no niggard of my cunning:
Come away.   Exeunt.

Enter Clowne, Dick, Horse-courser, and a Carter.

Cart. Come my Maisters, I'le bring you to the best beere
n Europe, what ho, Hostis; where be these Whores?
Enter Hostis.

Host. How now, what lacke you? What my old Guesse
welcome.

Clow. Sirra Dick, dost thou know why I stand so mute?

Dick. No Robin, why is't?

Clow. I am eightéene pence on the score, but say nothing,
see if she haue forgotten me.

Host. Who's this, that stands so solemnly by himselfe:
what my old Guest?

Clo. O Hostisse how do you? I hope my score stands still.

Host. I there's no doubt of that, for me thinkes you make
no hast to wipe it out.

Dick. Why Hostesse, I say, fetch vs some Béere. (Exit.

Host. You shall presently: looke vp into th'hall there ho.

Dick. Come sirs, what shall we do now till mine Hostesse
omes?

Cart. Marry sir, I'le tell you the brauest tale how a Con-
urer seru'd me; you know Doctor Fauster.

Horse. I, a plague take him, heere's some on's hane cause
o know him; did he coniure thee too?

Cart. I'le tell you how he seru'd me: As I was going to
Wittenberge t'other day, with a loade of Hay, he met me,
and asked me what he should giue me for as much Hay as he
could eate; now sir, I thinking that a little would serue his
turne, bad him take as much as he would for three-farthings;
so he presently gaue me my mony, and fell to eating; and as I
am a cursen man, he neuer left eating, till he had eate vp all
my loade of hay.

All. O monstrous, eate a whole load of Hay!

Clow:

Clow. Yes, yes, that may be; for I haue heard of one, that ha's eate a load of logges.

Horse. Now sirs, you shall heare how villanously he seru'd mee: I went to him yesterday to buy a horse of him, and he would by no meanes sell him vnder 40 Dollors; so sir, because I knew him to be such a horse, as would run ouer hedge and ditch, and neuer tyre, I gaue him his money; so when I had my horse, Doctor Fauster bad me ride him night and day, and spare him no time; but, quoth he, in any case ride him not into the water. Now sir, I thinking the horse had had some quality that he would not haue me know of, what did I but rid him into a great riuer, and when I came iust in the midst my horse vanisht away, and I sate straddling vpon a bottle of Hay.

All. O braue Doctor.

Horse. But you shall heare how brauely I seru'd him for it; I went me home to his house, and there I found him asleepe; I kept a hallowing and whooping in his eares, but all could not wake him: I seeing that, tooke him by the leg, and neuer rested pulling, till I had pul'd me his leg quite off, and now 'tis at home in mine Hostry.

Clow. And has the Doctor but one leg then? that's excellent, for one of his deuils turn'd me, into the likenesse of an Apes face.

Cart. Some more drinke Hostesse.

Clow. Hearke you, we'le into another roome and drinke a while, and then we'le go seeke out the Doctor.

Exeunt omnes.

Enter the Duke of Vanholt; his Dutches, Faustus, and Mephostophilis.

Duke. Thankes Maister Doctor, for these pleasant sights, Nor know I how sufficiently to recompence your great deserts in erecting that inchanted Castle in the Aire: the Sight whereof so delighted me, As nothing in the world could please me more.

Faust.

48

Fauſt. I do thinke my ſelfe my good Lord, highly recom-penced, in that it pleaſeth your grace to thinke but well of that which Fauſtus hath performed. But gratious Lady, it may be, that you haue taken no pleaſure in thoſe ſights; therefor I pray you tell me, what is the thing you moſt deſire to haue, be it in the world, it ſhall be yours: I haue heard that great bellyed women, do long for things, are rare and dainty.

Lady. True Maiſter Doctor, and ſince I finde you ſo kind I will make knowne vnto you what my heart deſires to haue, and were it now Summer, as it is Ianuary, a dead time of the Winter, I would requeſt no better meate, then a diſh of ripe grapes.

Fau. This is but a ſmall matter: Go Mephoſtophilis, away.

Exit Mephoſto.

Madam, I will do more then this for your content.

Enter Mepho. agen with the grapes.

Here, now taſte yee theſe, they ſhould be good for they come from a farre Country I can tell you.

Duke. This makes me wonder more then all the reſt, that this time of the yeare, when euery Tree is barren of his fruite, from whence you had theſe ripe grapes.

Fauſt. Pleaſe it your grace, the yeare is diuided into two circles ouer the whole world, ſo that when it is Winter with vs, in the contrary circle it is likewiſe Summer with them, as in India, Saba, and ſuch Countries that lye farre Eaſt, where they haue fruit twice a yeare. From whence, by meanes of a ſwift ſpirit that I haue, I had theſe grapes brought as you ſee.

Lady And truſt me, they are the ſweeteſt grapes that ere I taſted.

The Clowne bounce at the gate, within.

Duke. What rude diſturbers haue we at the gate?

G   Go

49

The Tragicall Historie

Go pacifie their fury set it ope,
And then demand of them, what they would haue.

They knocke againe, and call out to talke with Faustus.

A Seruant. Why how now Maisters, what a coyle is
there?
What is the reason you disturbe the Duke?

Dick. We haue no reason for it, therefore a fig for him.

Ser. Why saucy varlets, dare you be so bold.

Horse. I hope sir, we haue wit enough to be more bold
then welcome.

Ser. It appeares so, pray be bold else-where,
And trouble not the Duke.

Duke. What would they haue?

Ser. They all cry out to speake with Doctor Faustus.

Cart. I, and we will speake with him,

Duke. Will you sir? Commit the Rascals.

Dick. Commit with vs, he were as good commit with his
father, as commit with vs.

Faust. I do beseech your grace let them come in,
They are good subiect for a merriment.

Duke. Do as thou wilt Faustus, I giue thee leaue.

Faust. I thanke your grace:

*Enter the Clowne, Dick, Carter, and
Horse-courser.*

Why, how now my goods friends?
Faith you are too outragious, but come neere,
I haue procur'd your pardons: welcome all.

Clow. Nay sir, we will be wellcome for our mony, and
we will pay for what we take: What ho, giue's halfe a do-
sen of Beere here, and be hang'd.

Faust. Nay, hearke you, can you tell me where you are?

Cart. I marry can I, we are vnder heauen.

Ser. I but sir sauce box, know you in what place?

Horse

50

Horſc. I, I, the house is good enough to dꝛink in: Zons
fill vs some Beere, oꝛ we'll bꝛeake all the barrels in the houſe,
and daſh out all your bꝛaines with your Bottles.

Fauſ. Be not ſo furious: come you ſhall haue Beere.
My Loꝛd, beſeech you giue me leaue a while,
I'le gage my credit, 'twill content your grace.

Duke. With all my heart kind Docto;, pleaſe thy ſelfe,
Our ſeruants, and our Courts at thy command.

Fauſt. I humbly thanke your grace: then fetch ſome
Beere.

Horſc. I mary, there ſpake a Doctoꝛ indeed, and 'faith Ile
dꝛinke a health to thy woodden leg foꝛ that woꝛd.

Fauſt. My woodden leg? what doſt thou meane by that?

Cart. Ha, ha, ha, doſt heare him Dick, he has foꝛgot his
legge.

Horſc. I, I, he does not ſtand much vpon that.

Fauſt. No faith, not much vpon a woodden leg.

Cart. Good Loꝛd, that fleſh and bloud ſhould be ſo fraile
with your Woꝛſhip: Do not you remember a Hoꝛſe-courſer
you ſold a hoꝛſe to?

Fauſt. Yes, I remember I ſold one a hoꝛſe.

Cart. And do you remember you bid he ſhould not ride
into the water?

Fauſt. Yes, I do verie well remember that.

Cart. And do you remember nothing of your leg?

Fauſt. No in good ſooth.

Cart. Then I pꝛay remember your curteſie.

Fauſt. I thank you ſir.

Car. 'Tis not ſo much woꝛth; I pꝛay you tel me one thing.

Fauſt. What's that?

Cart. Be both your legs bedfellowes euery nig'ht together?

Fauſt. Wouldſt thou make a Coloſſus of me, that thou aſ-
keſt me ſuch queſtions?

Cart. No truelie ſir, I would make nothing of you, but
I would faine know that.

Enter Hoſteſſe with drinke.

Fauſt. Then I aſſure thee certainelie they are.

Cart.

Cart. I thanke you, I am fully satiffied.

Fauft. But wherefore doft thou afke?

Cart. For nothing fir: but me thinkes you fhould haue a wooden bedfellow of one of 'em.

Horfc. Why do you heare fir, did not I pull off one of your legs when you were afleepe?

Fauft. But I haue it againe now I am awake: looke you heere fir.

All. O horrible, had the Doctor three legs.

Cart. Do you remember fir, how you cofened me and eat vp my load of ——

Fauftus charmes him dumb.

Dick. Do you remember how you made me weare an Apes ——

Horfc. You whorefon coniuring fcab, do you remember how yo cofened me with a ho ——

Clow. Ha' you forgotten me? you thinke to carry it away with your Hey-paffe, and Re-paffe: do you remember the dogs fa ——

Exeunt Clownes.

Hoft. Who payes for the Ale? heare you Maifter Doctor, now you haue fent away my gueffe, I pray who fhall pay me for my A —— ?

Exit Hofteffe.

Lady. My Lord,
We are much beholding to this learned man.

Duke. So are we Madam, which we will recompence
With all the loue and kindneffe that we may.
His Artfull fport, driues all fad thoughts away.

Exeunt.

Thunder and lightning: Enter deuils with couer'd
diſhes: Mephoſtophilis leades them into
Fauſtus Study: Then enter
Wagner.

Wag. I think my Maifter means to die fhortly, he has made his will, & giuen me his wealth, his house, his goods, & ſtore of golden

golden plate; beſides two thouſand duckets ready coin'd : J wonder what he meanes, if death were nie, he would not fro-lick thus : hæe's now at ſupper with the ſchollers, where they'r ſuch belly-chæere, as Wagner in his life nere ſaw the like : and ſæ where they come, belike the feaſt is done.   Exit.

Enter Fauſtus, Mephoſtophilis, and two or three
Schollers.

1. Schol. M. Docto2 Fauſtus, ſince our conference about faire Ladies, which was the beautifulleſt in all the wo2ld, we haue determin'd with our ſelues, that Hellen of Græce was the admirableſt Lady that euer liu'd : therefo2e M. Docto2, if you will doe vs ſo much fauour, as to let vs ſæ that pæereleſſe dame of Græce, whom all the wo2ld admires fo2 Maieſty, we hould thinke our ſelues much beholding vnto you.

Fauſt. Gentlemen, fo2 ẏ J know your friendſhip is vnfain'd,
Jt is not Fauſtus cuſtome to deny
The iuſt requeſt of thoſe that wiſh him well :
Dou ſhall behold that pæreleſſe dame of Græce,
Do otherwiſe fo2 pompe o2 Maieſty,
Then when ſir Paris croſt the ſeas with her,
Jnd b2ought the ſpoyles to rich Dardania :
Be ſilent then, fo2 danger is in wo2ds.

Muſicke ſound, Mephoſto brings in Hellen, ſhe paſſeth
ouer the ſtage.

2 VVas this faire Hellen, whoſe admired wo2th
Made Greece with ten yeares warres afflict po2e Troy?
3 To ſimple is my wit to tell her wo2th,
Whom all the wo2ld admires fo2 maieſty.
1 Now we haue ſeene the p2ide of Natures wo2ke,
Wee'l take our leaues, and fo2 this bleſſed ſight
Dappy and bleſt be Fauſtus euermo2e.   Exeunt Schollers.
Fauſt. Gentlemen farewell : the ſame with J to you.

G 3.   Enter

Enter an old Man.

Old Man. O gentle Faustus leaue this damned Art,
This Magicke, that will charme thy soule to hell,
And quite bereaue thee of saluation.
Though thou hast now offended like a man,
Doe not perseuer in it like a Diuell;
Yet, yet, thou hast an amiable soule,
If sin by custome grow not into nature: 1830
Then Faustus, will repentance come too late,
Then thou art banisht from the sight of heauen;
No mortall can expresse the paines of hell.
It may be this my exhortation
Seemes harsh, and all vnpleasant; let it not,
For gentle sonne, I speake it not in wrath,
Or enuy of thee, but in tender loue,
And pitty of thy future miserie.
And so haue hope, that this my kinde rebuke,
Checking thy body, may amend thy soule.
Faust. Where art thou Faustus? wretch, what hast thou done?   1840
Hell claimes his right, & with a roaring voyce,   Meph. giues
Saies Faustus come, thine houre is almost come,   him a dag-
And Faustus now will come to do thee right.   ger.
Old. O stay good Faustus, stay thy desperate steps.
I see an Angell houer ore thy head,
And with a vyoll full of pretious grace,
Offers to poure the same into thy soule,
Then call for mercy, and auoyd despaire.
Fa. O friend, I feele thy words to comfort my distressed soule,
Leaue me a while, to ponder on my sinnes.   1850
Old. Faustus I leaue thee, but with griefe of heart,
Fearing the enemy of thy haplesse soule.   Exit.
Faust. Accursed Faustus, wretch what hast thou done?
I do repent, and yet I doe despaire,
Hell striues with grace for conquest in my breast:
What shall I doe to shun the snares of death?
Meph. Thou traytor Faustus, I arrest thy soule,
For disobedience to my soueraigne Lord,

Reuolt

54

Reuolt, o2 I'le in peece-meale teare thy flesh.

Fauft. I do repent I ere offended him,
Sweet Mephafto: intreat thy Lo2d
To pardon my bniuft p2efumption,
And with my bloud againe I will confirme
The former vow I made to Lucifer.
Do it then Fauftus, with bnfained heart,
Left greater dangers do attend thy d2ift.
To2ment fweet friend, that bafe and aged man,
That durft diffwade me from thy Lucifer,
With greateft to2ment that our hell affo02ds.

Meph. His faith is great, I cannot touch his foule;
But what I may afflict his body with,
I will attempt, which is but little wo2th.

Fauft. One thing good feruant let me craue of thee,
To glut the longing of my hearts defire,
That I may haue vnto my paramour,
That heauenly Hellen, which I faw of late,
Whofe fweet emb2aces may extinguifh cleare,
Thofe thoughts that do diffwade me from my vow,
And keepe my vow I made to Lucifer.

Meph. This, o2 what elfe my Fauftus fhall defire,
Shall be perfo2m'd in twinkling of an eye.

Enter Hellen againe, paffing ouer betweene
two Cupids.

Fauft. Was this the face that Launcht a thoufand fhips,
And burnt the topleffe Towers of Ilium?
Sweet Hellen make me immo2tall with a kiffe:
Her lips fucke fo2th my foule, fee where it flies.
Come Hellen, come, giue me my foule againe,
Here will I dwell, fo2 heauen is in thefe lippes,
And all is d2offe that is not Helena.
I will be Paris, and fo2 loue of thee,
In ftead of Troy fhall Wittenberg be fack't,
And I will combat with weake Menelaus,
And weare thy colours on my plumed creft.

Yea,

55

Yea, I will wound Achilles in the heele,
And then returne to Hellen for a kisse.
O thou art fairer then the euenings aire,
Clad in the beauty of a thousand starres:
Brighter art thou then flaming Iupiter,
When he appear'd to haplesse Semele:
More louely then the Monarch of the sky,
In wanton Arethusa's azure armes,
And none but thou shalt be my Paramour.　　Exeunt.

Thunder.　Enter Lucifer, Belzebub, and Mephostophilis.

Lucif. Thus from infernall Dis do we ascend
To view the subiects of our Monarchy,
Those soules which sinne, seales the blacke sonnes of hell,
'Mong which as chiefe, Faustus we come to thee,
Bringing with vs lasting damnation,
To wait vpon thy soule; the time is come
Which makes it forfeit.
　　Meph. And this gloomy night,
Here in this roome will wretched Faustus be.
　　Bels. And here wee'l stay,
To marke him how he doth demeane himselfe.
　　Meph. How should he, but in desperate lunacie.
Fond worldling, now his heart bloud dries with griefe;
His conscience kils it, and his labouring braine,
Begets a world of idle fantasies,
To ouer-reach the Diuell; but all in paine,
His store of pleasures must be sauc'd with paine.
He and his seruant Wagner are at hand,
Both come from drawing Faustus latest will.
See where they come.　　　Enter Faustus and Wagner.
　　Faust. Say Wagner, thou hast perus'd my will,
How dost thou like it?
　　Wag. Sir, so wondrous well,
As in all humble dutie, I do yeeld
My life and lasting seruice for your loue.　Enter the scholers.
　　　　　　　　　　　　　　　　　　　　　　　　Faust.

56

Fauſt. Gramercies Wagner. Welcome gentlemen.

1 Now worthy Fauſtus: me thinks your looks are chang'd.

Fauſt. Oh gentlemen.

2. What ailes Fauſtus?

Fauſt. Ah my ſwéet chamber-fellow, had I liu'd with thee, Then had I liued ſtill, but now muſt dye eternally. Looke ſirs, comes he not, comes he not?

1. O my déere Fauſtus what imports this feare?

2. Is all our pleaſure turn'd to melancholy?

3. He is not well with being ouer ſolitarie.

2 If it be ſo, wée'l haue Phyſitians, and Fauſtus ſhall bee cur'd.

3 Tis but a ſurfet ſir, feare nothing.

Fauſt. A ſurfet of deadly ſin, that hath damn'd both body and ſoule.

2 Yet Fauſtus looke vp to heauen, and remember mercy is infinite.

Fauſt. But Fauſtus offence can nere be pardoned, The ſerpent that tempted Eue may be ſaued, But not Fauſtus. O gentlemen heare with patience, and trem-ble not at my ſpéeches, though my heart pant & quiuer to re-member that I haue béene a ſtudent here theſe 30 yeares. O would I had neuer ſeene Wittenberg, neuer read book, & what wonders I haue done, all Germany can witneſſe: yea all the world, for which Fauſtus hath loſt both Germany & the world, yea heauen it ſelfe: heauen the ſeate of God, the Throne of the Bleſſed, the kingdome of Ioy, and muſt remaine in hell for euer. Hell, O hell for euer. Sweet friends, what ſhall be-come of Fauſtus being in hell for euer?

2 Yet Fauſtus call on God.

Fauſt. On God, whom Fauſtus hath abiur'd? on God, whom Fauſtus hath blaſphem'd? O my God, I would wéepe, but the Diuell drawes in my teares. Guſh forth bloud in ſtead of teares, yea life and ſoule: oh hée ſtayes my tongue: I would lift vp my hands, but ſee they hold 'em, they hold 'em.

All. Who Fauſtus?

Fauſt. Why Lucifer and Mephoſtophilis: O gentlemen,

H   I

I gaue them my soule for my cunning.

   All. O God forbid.

   Fauſt. God forbade it indéd, but Fauſtus hath done it: for the vaine pleaſure of foure and twenty yeares hath Fauſtus loſt eternall ioy and felicitie. I writ them a bill with mine owne bloud, the date is expired: this is the time, and he will fetch mé.

   1 Why did not Fauſtus tell vs of this before, that Diuines might haue prayd for thee?

   Fauſt. Oft haue I thought to haue done ſo: but the Diuel threatned to teare me in peeces if I nam'd God: to fetch me body and ſoule, if I once gaue eare to Diuinitie: and now 'ts too late. Gentlemen away, leaſt you periſh with me.

   2 O what may we do to ſaue *Fauſtus*?

   Fauſt. Talke not of me, but ſaue your ſelues and depart.

   3. God will ſtrengthen me, I will ſtay with *Fauſtus.*

   1. Tempt not God ſweet friend, but let vs into the next roome, and pray for him.

   Fauſt. I, pray for me, pray for me: and what noyſe ſoeuer you heare, come not vnto me, for nothing can reſcue me.

   2. Pray thou, and we will pray, that God may haue mercie vpon thee.

   Fauſt. Gentlemen farewell: if I liue till morning, I'le viſit you: if not, Fauſtus is gone to hell.

   All. Fauſtus, farewell.   *Exeunt Schollers.*

   Meph. I Fauſtus, now thou haſt no hope of heauen, Therefore deſpaire, thinke onely vpon hell; For that muſt be thy manſion, there to dwell.

   Fauſt. O thou bewitching fiend, 'twas thy temptation, Hath rob'd me of eternall happineſſe.

   Meph. I doe confeſſe it Fauſtus, and reioyce; 'Twas I, that when thou wer't i'the way to heauen, Damb'd vp thy paſſage, when thou took'ſt the booke, To view the Scriptures, then I turn'd the leaues And led thine eye. What weep'ſt thou? 'tis too late, deſpaire, farewell,

Foole

Fooles that will laugh on earth, moſt weepe in hell. Exit

Enter the good Angell, and the bad Angell at
ſeuerall doores.

Good. Oh Fauſtus, if thou hadſt giuen eare to me,
Innumerable ioyes had followed thee.
But thou didſt loue the world.

Bad. Gaue eare to me,
And now muſt taſte hels paines perpetually.

Good. O what will all thy riches,pleaſures,pompes,
Auaile thee now?

Bad. Nothing but vere thee moze,
To want in hell,that had on earth ſuch ſtoze.

Muſicke while the Throne deſcends.

Good. O thou haſt loſt celeſtiall happineſſe,
Pleaſures vnſpeakeable, bliſſe without end.
Hadſt thou affected ſweet diuinitie,
Hell,oz the Diuell, had had no power on thee.
Hadſt thou kept on that way, Fauſtus behold,
In what reſplendant glozy thou hadſt ſet
In yonder thzone,like thoſe bzight ſhining Saints,
And triumpht ouer hell, that haſt thou loſt,
And now poze ſoule muſt thy good Angell leaue thee,
The iawes of hell are open to receiue thee. Exit.

Hell is diſcouered.

Bad. Now Fauſtus let thine eyes with hozroz ſtare
Into that vaſte perpetuall tozture-houſe,
There are the Furies toſſing damned ſoules,
On burning fozkes : their bodies bzoyle in lead.
There are liue quarters bzoyling on the coles,
That ner'e can die: this euer-burning chaire,
Is foz oze-toztur'd ſoules to reſt them in.
Theſe,that are fed with ſoppes of flaming fire,
Were gluttons,and lou'd only delicates,
And laught to ſee the poze ſtarue at their gates:
But yet all theſe are nothing,thou ſhalt ſee

H 2   Ten

59

ten thousand tortures that more horrid be.

Faust. O, I haue seene enough to torture me.

Bad. Nay, thou must feele them, taste the smart of all.
He that loues pleasure, must for pleasure fall :
And so I leaue thee Faustus till anon,
Then wilt thou tumble in confusion.   Exit.

                The Clock strikes eleuen.

Faust. O Faustus
Now hast thou but one bare houre to liue,
And then thou must be damn'd perpetually.
Stand still you euer mouing Spheares of heauen,
That time may cease, and midnight neuer come.
Faire natures eye, rise, rise againe and make
Perpetuall day : or let this houre be but a yeare,
A month, a weeke, a naturall day,
That Faustus may repent, and saue his soule.
O lente lente currite noctis equi :
The Stars moue still, Time runs, the Clocke will strike.
The deuill will come, and Faustus must be damn'd.
O I'le leape vp to heauen : who puls me downe?
One drop of bloud will saue me; oh my Christ,
Rend not my heart, for naming of my Christ.
Yet will I call on him : O spare me Lucifer.
Where is it now? 'tis gone.
And see a threatning Arme, an angry Brow.
Mountaines and Hils, come, come, and fall on me,
And hide me from the heauy wrath of heauen.
No? Then will I headlong run into the earth:
Gape earth; O no, it will not harbour me.
You Starres that raign'd at my natiuity,
Whose influence hath allotted death and hell;
Now draw vp Faustus like a foggy mist,
Into the entrals of yon labouring cloud,
That when you vomite forth into the aire,
My limbes may issue from your smoky mouthes,
But let my soule mount, and ascend to heauen.

                The Watch strikes.

O halfe the houre is past: 'twill all be past anone:
O, if my soule must suffer for my sinne,
Impose some end to my incessant paine:

Let Faustus liue in hell a thousand yeares,
A hundred thousand, and at last be sau'd.
No end is limited to damned soules.
Why wert thou not a creature wanting soule?
Or why is this immortall that thou hast?
Oh Pythagoras Metemsycosis; were that true,
This soule should flie from me, and I be chang'd
Into some brutish beast.
All beasts are happy, for when they die,

Their soules are soone dissolu'd in elements,
But mine must liue still to be plagu'd in hell.
Curst be the parents that ingendred me;
No Faustus, curse thy selfe, curse Lucifer,
That hath depriu'd thee of the ioies of heauen.
                              The clocke strikes twelue

It strikes, it strikes; now body turne to aire,
Or Lucifer will beare thee quicke to hell.
O soule be chang'd into small water drops,
and fall into the Ocean ne're be found.
                    Thunder, and enter the deuils.

O mercy heauen, looke not so fierce on me;
Adders and serpents let me breathe a while:
Ugly hell gape not; come not Lucifer,
I'le burne my bookes; oh Mephostophilis.   Exeunt.

Enter the Schollers.

  1 Come Gentlemen, let vs go visit Faustus,
For such a dreadfull night, was neuer seene,
Since first the worlds creation did begin.
Such fearefull shrikes, and cries, were neuer heard,
Pray heauen the Doctor haue escapt the danger.
  2 O help vs heauen, see, here are Faustus limbs,
All torne asunder by the hand of death.

                              P 3   3 The

61

3 The deuils whom Faustus seru'd haue torne him thus:
For twixt the houres of twelue and one, methought
I heard him shreeke and call aloud for helpe:
At which selfe time the house seem'd all on fire,
With dreadfull horror of these damned fiends.

2 Well Gentlemen, tho Faustus end be such
As euery Christian heart laments to thinke on:
Yet for he was a Scholler, once admired
For wondrous knowledge in our Germane schooles,
We'll giue his mangled limbs due buryall:
And all the Students clothed in mourning blacke,
Shall waite vpon his heauy funerall.   *Exeunt.*

Enter Chorus.

Cut is the branch that might haue growne full straight,
And burned is Apollo's Lawrell bough,
That some time grew within this learned man,
Faustus is gone, regard his hellish fall,
Whose fiendfull fortune may exhort the wise
Onely to wonder at vnlawfull things:
Whose deepnesse doth intice such forward wits,
To practise more then heauenly power permits.

Terminat hora diem, Terminat Author opus.

FINIS.